GW00703365

THE DETERMINANTS OF IRISH IMPORTS

Copies of this paper may be obtained from The Economic and Social Research Institute (Limited Company No. 182681). Registered Office: 4 Burlington Road, Dublin 4.

Price IR£8.00

(Special rate for students IR£4.00)

John D. FitzGerald is a Senior Research Officer with The Economic and Social Research Institute. The Paper has been accepted for publication by the Institute, which is not responsible for either the content, or the views expressed therein.

THE DETERMINANTS OF
IRISH IMPORTS

JOHN D. FITZGERALD

© THE ECONOMIC AND SOCIAL RESEARCH INSTITUTE
DUBLIN, 1987

ISBN 0 7070 0093 9

Acknowledgements

The author would like to thank Dr J. Bradley and Dr P. Bacon for their many helpful comments on earlier drafts of this paper. Many other members of the staff of the ESRI contributed to this report at various stages of its development. Michael McDonnell, Noel O'Gorman, Dave Hurley and other individuals in the Department of Finance and the Central Bank provided much helpful advice, criticism, and encouragement throughout this project. An anonymous referee brought to the author's attention a number of important points which had escaped his notice. As usual, the author is solely responsible for any errors and omissions in the paper.

CONTENTS

LIST OF TABLES

LIST OF FIGURES

GENERAL SUMMARY

Background

Since the foundation of the State the size of Ireland's merchandise import bill has been a central issue for those interested in economic policy. Over the years much attention has been given to its magnitude and to ways in which it could be reduced. Up to 1984 imports exceeded exports in every year since the end of the Second World War and major economic crises were characterised by a rise in the balance of payments deficit to what was felt to be an unsustainable level. The standard policy response was to restrain domestic demand to reduce the level of imports. It is a sign of how much has changed in the Irish economy that so little attention has been given in the last three years to the reversal in this traditional excess of imports over exports. To an economy watcher of the 1960s looking at the Irish economy today this reversal in the chronic deficit in the balance of trade would be a major surprise, though the plethora of other novel and disturbing economic problems would soon distract attention. Nevertheless, the alteration in the structure of the economy which has brought about this change in the balance of trade is clearly of major importance. It is important to establish why the change has taken place; whether it is due to a slow-down in economic activity and whether there would be an explosion of imports if the rate of economic growth were to rise. To answer these questions it is necessary to look anew at the determinants of the volume of Irish imports.

While merchandise imports have risen less rapidly than merchandise exports, they still rose much faster than the other components of final demand due to a continuing high propensity to import. This paper examines this rising share of imports in final demand over the period 1960 to 1982 and considers a range of different factors which may have caused it. Among the potential factors are changes in the pattern of domestic demand in favour of goods with a high import content; changes in the competitiveness of Irish industry; the freeing of trade under the Anglo-Irish Free Trade Agreement and Ireland's entry into the EEC; and the effects of domestic fiscal policy raising the level of capacity utilisation in the domestic economy. To help identify the relative importance of these different factors imports have been broken down into six different categories which are examined separately.

1

Results

The results of this study indicate that changes in the pattern of demand in favour of goods with a high import content have been a major factor in the increased import penetration of the Irish economy over the past twenty-five years: there was a rapid increase in the capital stock, much of which consisted of imported machinery and equipment; the major growth in the industrial sector centred around the extensive use of imported raw materials (the propensity to import out of industrial exports is quite high); increasing wealth has led consumers to seek a wider choice of products and to devote an increasing share of their incomes to goods which are not produced in Ireland (e.g., cars and avocado pears). All of these factors would have resulted in a substantial increase in import penetration even if there had been no change in the competitive position of the Irish economy over the period. The research results presented in the paper indicate that approximately half of the rise in manufactured import penetration and a quarter of the rise in total import penetration was attributable to this change in the composition of demand.

The results of this study show that the volume of imports is affected by the competitiveness of Irish industry; changes in the price of imports relative to the price of other inputs, especially that of labour, have significantly increased the propensity to import over the period examined. Changes in the capital intensity of industrial output affect the volume of imports. Imports are also subject to strong cyclical variation; when output is below its expected long-run level imports decline and when output is pushed above trend much of the additional demand is met from imports.

In the short term, the effects on imports of changes in competitiveness, in particular wage cost competitiveness, are relatively small: a 1.0 per cent rise in wage rates leads to a rise in imports of between 0.13 per cent and 0.21 per cent. Over time, however, the cumulative effects are quite large. This study suggests that the deterioration in labour cost competitiveness had a major effect on the propensity to import throughout the period. This is especially so for the 1960s. In the case of manufactured imports we found that this loss of competitiveness probably accounted for nearly half of the observed rise in the propensity to import out of final demand over the period 1960-82. In addition, any long-run effects of the disimprovement in competitiveness on the productive capacity must be added to these cumulative short-run effects to arrive at the final effect on the economy. The evidence from another study (Bradley and FitzGerald, 1987) suggests that this cumulative long-run effect on productive capacity can be quite large.

EEC entry had its biggest effect on imports of food. It is estimated that, by the end of the period, food imports were at least a quarter higher than they would have been under the trading regime in force prior to EEC entry.

In the case of manufactured imports no significant impact of EEC entry was detected. This does not mean that the elimination of customs' duties had no effect but rather that any such effect was relatively small when compared to the results of other changes in the economy over the same period.

This paper makes clear the importance of domestic supply factors in determining the level of imports. If the productive capacity is not there to supply domestic needs or if it is not profitable to supply them by domestic production, imports fill the gap.

Results for Categories of Imports

Food: Food imports rose by between a quarter and a half as a result of EEC entry. This does not necessarily mean that the economy suffered as a result of this increase: account must be taken of the wider choice made available to consumers through the reduction of import controls and also of the effects of farmers switching production to exports where profitability was enhanced through EEC entry. The effects of EEC entry on the propensity to import food were completed by the early 1980s and the propensity to import should stabilise over the rest of the decade. As living standards improve a smaller share of income will probably go on food, including food imports. While any increase in domestic agricultural output generally reduced food imports, this effect was small by the end of the period; the Irish agricultural sector shifted its capacity to producing for export rather than home markets.

Energy: The volume of energy imports is influenced by changes in relative prices. It is estimated that the long-run effect of a 1 per cent rise in energy prices in 1982 would have been to reduce energy demand by around 0.6 per cent. The economy takes a long time to adjust to changes in real energy prices. The failure to take account of this slow speed of adjustment may have accounted for the failure to detect significant price elasticities in many earlier studies.

Manufactured Goods: Just over half the rise in the propensity to import manufactured goods over the period 1960 to 1982 was due to changes in the composition of demand in favour of goods with a high import content. The rapid rise in rates of pay in industry compared to the cost of imported manufactured goods was the other major factor in the rise in the propensity to import over time. This was of particular importance in the 1960s. The propensity to import out of industrial exports was very high at around a half. A 1 per cent change in the price of imports would reduce the volume of imports by about 0.25 per cent. The elasticity with respect to wage rates was just under 0.2. We found that any change in capacity utilisation results in a substantial change in the volume of imports.

Services: The study suggests that expenditure abroad by Irish tourists will tend to rise faster than income. It also suggests that this expenditure is sensitive to the price of some domestic services.

Policy Conclusions

1. The first major policy question which arises from these results concerns what is likely to happen to the propensity to import in the future. The change in the pattern of demand, which was so important a factor in the rise in the propensity in the past, is likely to be less important in the future. Exports and investment in machinery and equipment, which have a high import content, are unlikely to increase their share of final demand from their present high level.

Clearly, changes in the competitiveness of Irish industry could affect the propensity to import in the future. They played a significant role in raising the propensity to import in the 1960s, though their effects in the 1970s were somewhat smaller. In the absence of a compositional effect, the development of competitiveness in the future will be the major potential factor affecting the propensity to import.

2. The second major policy implication to be drawn from this study is that a stimulus to output from fiscal policy will result in a substantial rise in the propensity to import above its pre-existing level. The multiplier effects of such stimuli will, as a result, be small. This is in line with the results of a number of other studies. Even as a short-term demand management measure, demand stimuli to the Irish economy will have little effect on output and employment, serving only to raise capacity utilisation and imports. For example, if capacity utilisation in 1982 had been raised to its 1979 level by a fiscal stimulus, imports would have been almost 10 per cent above their actual level.

3. The third major policy question which arises from this study is the magnitude of the benefits to the Irish economy from the growth in industrial exports. The estimated propensity to import out of a unit change in industrial exports is very high. When taken together with the large repatriation of profits by foreign owned companies, this implies that the true domestic value added is not very great. While it is clear that, even with a small domestic content,

the growth of exports is the only way to promote the long-term growth of the economy, it is, none the less, a major cause for concern whether we are paying too much in terms of subsidies and tax write offs for these exports.

4. The fourth major question which arises from this study concerns energy imports. The results indicate that, in forecasting future energy demand, it is important to take account of changes in relative prices. Large and costly mistakes will be made if this is not done in the future. The economy takes a long time to adjust to relative price changes and is still adjusting to changes in prices which took place in the 1970s. As a result, current trends in energy demand are not necessarily a good indicator of trends in the medium to long term.

In conclusion, it should be remarked that the increased import penetration of the Irish economy over the period examined was not necessarily a bad thing. It provided the machinery and equipment to increase our capital stock. It allowed the growth of many industries which relied on free access to imported materials (and free access to foreign markets). It helped meet consumer demands for products which could not be produced domestically. It is only in so far as it killed off industries producing for the domestic market that it may have carried a cost.

For the future the results of the study suggest that the propensity to import, through its effects on the balance of payments, will not pose as big a constraint on growth as it did in the past. Provided that the ill-fated policies of demand stimulation, popular over the 1970s and early 1980s, are avoided we can look forward to more balanced growth in the future. The problem of raising the Irish growth rate can only be tackled by policies which raise the output potential of the economy. This may be platitudinous but, in the light of past history, clearly needs repetition.

Chapter 1

SCOPE AND PURPOSE OF THE STUDY

1.1 *Introduction*

Since the foundation of the State the size of Ireland's import bill has been a central issue for those interested in economic policy. Over the years much attention has been given to its magnitude and to ways in which it could be reduced. Import substitution has been an objective of many governments over that period. This interest in the quantity of goods which we import is not surprising or unusual. As a small economy in a world where economies of scale are of vital importance in manufacturing industry, we have had to meet a large part of our requirements for consumer goods and capital goods by buying them on foreign markets. The way our industrial sector has developed since the 1930s with relatively little emphasis on the processing of domestic raw materials has accentuated this need to import a large volume of materials for further processing.

Due to the fact that imports exceeded exports in every year between the end of the Second World War and 1984 the volume of imports was a major preoccupation of policy makers throughout most of this forty year period. In the period up to the mid-1970s major economic crises were characterised by a rise in the balance of payments deficit, to what was felt to be an unsustainable level. The standard policy response was to take action either directly, or indirectly through reducing the level of domestic demand, to reduce the level of imports. It is a sign of how much has changed in the Irish economy that so little attention has been given to the reversal in this traditional excess of imports over exports in the last two years. To anyone looking at the Irish economy today from the standpoint of the 1960s this reversal in the chronic deficit in the balance of trade would be a major surprise. No doubt the plethora of other economic problems which would present themselves as novel and disturbing would soon distract attention. However, the alteration in the structure of the economy which has brought this about is clearly of major importance.

Because of the importance of imports in the Irish economy their behaviour was a frequent subject of economic research in the past. In the late 1960s and early 1970s quite a number of papers examined the behaviour of imports at both an aggregated and a disaggregated level (see Baker *et al.*, 1969/70 and

6

McAleese, 1970). The results of this research suggested that the marginal propensity to import in Ireland was substantially greater than the average propensity and that the elasticity of demand for imports with respect to domestic activity was substantially greater than one. It indicated that an ever increasing proportion of the growth in domestic economic activity would be met by imports. However, when the results of this research are confronted with the reality of the 1980s, there is a substantial overprediction of imports. It is important to establish why this change has taken place; whether it is due to a slowdown in economic activity and whether there would be an explosion of imports if the rate of growth in economic activity were to rise. To answer these questions it is necessary to look anew at the determinants of the volume of Irish imports. This paper describes the results of such a study.

The openness of the Irish economy and the importance of imports in both meeting consumer demand and as an input into the production process means that any study of imports must be cast within a wider framework. The previous studies of Irish imports have tended to ignore this wider context. In modelling the demand for imported materials by industry the fact that these are jointly determined with the other factors of production has generally been given little consideration. Similarly the demand for imported consumer goods has generally not been examined in the context of a model explaining the overall behaviour of consumers. (Exceptions to this are the studies by Geary and McDonnell, 1977 and 1980.) In this paper the wide range of factors which have potentially affected Irish imports over the period 1960 to 1982 are analysed within a wider model of the productive sector of the Irish economy. (An exception is the volume of tourism imports which is modelled as part of a consumer demand system.)

The most obvious factor affecting the growth of imports over the last quarter of a century has been the growth of the economy as a whole. However, as mentioned above, the growth of imports has been substantially faster than the overall growth in the economy reflecting a significant increase in import penetration. The potential factors which gave rise to this increased penetration are many. Among the more important which are considered in this study are: the opening of the Irish economy to trade as a result of the Anglo-Irish Free Trade Agreement in 1965 and Ireland's entry into the EEC in 1973; changes in the competitiveness of the Irish economy over the period as the cost of the factors of production in Ireland changed compared to those abroad; changes in the structure of the productive sector due to technical progress; and changes in consumer tastes as income rises. The objective of this paper is to analyse the relative importance of these different factors.

Section 1.2 of this chapter examines briefly the trend of total imports over the period of the study, 1960-1982. Section 1.3 considers the role of imports in the Irish economy using the information contained in successive input-output tables. Finally Section 1.4 spells out the structure of the rest of the paper.

1.2 *Trend of Imports*

As can be seen from Table 1.1 and Figure 1.1, throughout the period 1960 to 1980 the share of imports in final demand (all expressed at current prices) showed an upward trend. While there was a big step upwards in 1974 due to the rise in oil prices it was clear that there were other factors at work over the period which gave rise to an increase in the import penetration of the Irish economy. This is made clear by an examination of the share of imports in final demand, all expressed at constant 1980 prices (Table 1.1 and Figure 1.1). In using constant price data the direct effects of changes in the terms of trade on the share of imports is eliminated and a clearer picture emerges of the changing structure of the Irish economy over the period. The constant price data make it clear that the increase in import penetration was particularly rapid in the 1960s. While it continued in the 1970s the increase in penetration was much less than in the previous decade, in spite of the reduction in tariffs consequent on Ireland's entry into the EEC in 1973. In the early 1980s the share of imports in final demand fell in both current and constant price terms. This fall coincided with a prolonged period of stagnation in the economy.

Over the quarter of a century there were a number of important changes in the Irish economy which probably contributed to this growth in import penetration. In the 1930s a policy of developing Irish industry by protection was adopted. Much of the new industry was oriented towards supplying the domestic market. It was not until the mid-1960s that any significant change was made in this policy. As a result Ireland entered the 1960s with a relatively high level of tariff protection and a manufacturing sector which had developed for thirty years with the aid of this protection. Already by 1960 there had been a change in the direction of industrial policy. The introduction of export profits tax relief in 1956 and the provision of grant assistance to new foreign industry producing for export, presaged a new more outward-looking industrial policy. This policy, as implemented in the early 1960s, involved unilateral reductions in the protective tariff wall. As a result of this policy the protection given to Irish manufacturing industry was substantially reduced. The signing of the Anglo-Irish Free Trade Agreement in 1965 involved a further reduction in protection for certain sectors of Irish industry (McAleese, 1973). All of these changes made it much easier and cheaper to import a wide range of manufactured products from abroad than it had been in the previous decade. It is, therefore, not surprising that there was such a substantial increase in import penetration in the 1960s.

Table 1.1: *The Share of Total Imports in Final Demand*
(per cent)

	Current Prices	Constant Prices
1960	27.6	24.9
1961	29.0	26.7
1962	28.6	27.1
1963	29.6	28.3
1964	30.3	30.5
1965	30.5	31.2
1966	30.2	31.7
1967	29.1	31.5
1968	31.2	33.0
1969	31.7	34.7
1970	31.1	34.5
1971	30.3	34.7
1972	28.5	34.2
1973	30.9	37.2
1974	36.1	25.8
1975	32.8	32.8
1976	35.3	35.5
1977	37.2	36.6
1978	37.7	38.4
1979	40.2	40.9
1980	39.1	39.0
1981	39.1	38.8
1982	36.3	37.5

Source: Department of Finance Databank.

Ireland's entry into the EEC in 1973 involved the elimination of all protective tariffs and quotas with other EEC countries. The abolition of tariffs generally took place over a five year period. However, the reduction in protection in the 1960s in particular for trade with the UK, had already exposed the bulk of Irish manufacturing industry to competition from UK imports. The sectors of industry which were still protected to some extent against all foreign imports in 1973 were the food industry and the motor vehicle assembly industry. (In the case of the motor vehicle assembly industry protection was phased out over a ten year period after 1973.) It was to be expected that these sectors would be significantly affected by EEC entry. For the rest of industry, which was already subject to competition from the UK, it was not as clear how much domestic production would be replaced by new imports. In the event, the data shown in Table 1.1 suggest that EEC entry had less of an effect in increasing import penetration than did the freeing of trade in the

Figure 1.1: *Share of Total Imports in Final Demand*

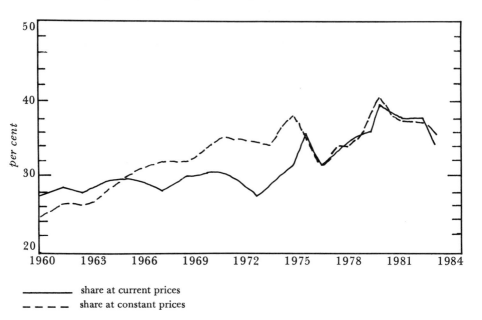

———————— share at current prices

— — — — share at constant prices

1960s. However, because of the many other factors at work over the period 1960-1982, it is not possible to reach any firm conclusions as to the effects of the reduction in barriers to trade on the level of import penetration without further research.

There was obviously a wide range of other factors affecting the demand for imports over the last quarter of a century. Among the more important were changes in the competitiveness of the Irish economy *vis-à-vis* foreign competitors; the growth in the overall standard of living leading to a change in the composition of demand in favour of a more varied range of goods and services; the growth of the Irish manufacturing sector with a major shift in favour of production for export rather than home markets. All of these factors are examined in later chapters of this paper.

The behaviour of imports in the early 1980s appears to show a different pattern from that experienced in the previous two decades. The share of imports in final demand, when considered in both value and volume terms, fell significantly in the early 1980s from its peak in 1979. Whether this represented a change in behaviour or whether it is readily explained by the prolonged recession in Ireland remains to be investigated in this paper. Obviously the answer to this question is of considerable importance for the future of the Irish economy in the medium term.

To better understand the behaviour of aggregate imports in Ireland this paper looks separately at the determinants of each of six different categories. In considering the results obtained from this analysis and its implications for the determinants of total imports, it is useful to examine the relative importance of each of the categories examined. As can be seen from Table 1.2, imports of manufactured goods, which accounted for just over 50 per cent by volume of total imports in 1960, had increased their share to 67 per cent by volume in 1982. As a result, the factors affecting this category of imports will be of major importance in explaining the movement of total imports over time. No other single category of imports accounted for more than one-eighth of the total in 1982.

Table 1.2: *Imports Disaggregated as a Percentage of Total Imports, Volume*

	Food	Raw Materials	Energy	Manufactured Goods	Services – Other	Services – Tourism
	SITC 0-1	SITC 2+4	SITC 3	SITC 5-9		
1960	14.2	8.4	18.4	50.8	1.6	6.6
1961	16.3	7.5	16.9	51.3	1.9	6.1
1962	15.0	7.5	15.7	53.5	1.7	6.5
1963	15.2	7.4	14.5	54.6	1.7	6.7
1964	13.7	6.9	13.0	58.1	2.1	6.3
1965	14.7	6.2	13.3	57.1	2.4	6.1
1966	13.7	6.1	13.6	57.2	3.0	6.5
1967	13.1	6.3	15.6	56.6	2.7	5.7
1968	12.6	6.6	13.2	59.0	2.9	5.7
1969	11.0	5.9	12.6	62.8	2.7	4.9
1970	11.0	5.9	14.4	61.5	2.5	4.7
1971	10.3	5.8	15.6	61.4	2.4	4.4
1972	11.5	5.9	13.7	62.4	2.3	4.2
1973	10.2	6.0	12.8	64.8	2.1	4.0
1974	11.0	6.0	12.4	64.4	2.0	4.3
1975	12.3	4.3	13.2	60.7	4.5	5.1
1976	11.8	4.9	11.2	63.5	4.3	4.4
1977	11.1	4.1	10.8	65.0	4.7	4.2
1978	10.1	3.7	9.6	67.0	5.0	4.6
1979	10.5	3.8	9.4	67.3	4.2	4.9
1980	11.1	3.6	9.6	66.4	4.4	4.9
1981	12.2	3.7	8.4	67.1	4.2	4.4
1982	12.0	3.5	8.3	67.3	4.7	4.3

Source: CSO Trade Statistics of Ireland.

1.3 *Imports and the Structure of the Irish Economy*

The three input-output (I-O) tables prepared by the CSO for 1964, 1969 and 1975 provide an important source of information on the structure of the Irish economy, in general, and on the role of imports in the economy, in particular. These tables provide a snapshot of the structure of the economy at three different points of time showing the sectors which had a relatively high import content in those years and showing what proportion of imports entered directly into final demand and what proportion first underwent trans-formation in the domestic productive sector. While these tables are purely a set of accounting identities and have no behavioural content (they do not explain why imports played the role they did in the economy) they do provide a valuable tool. They show which sectors of the economy played a crucial role in determining the demand for imports and they also provide an indication of what components of final demand had the highest import contents. (This information can be derived on the restrictive assumption that the proportion of each input used by each sector, as defined in the input-output table, is identical for each unit of output.) Finally, even though there are only three I-O tables available prepared by the CSO they do allow us to carry out a limited examination of how, though not why, the role of imports in the economy has changed over time. The origins of the tables and the preliminary analysis carried out on them is described in detail in Appendix 1. Here we only consider the results of this analysis.

As described in the Appendix, the I-O tables were used to derive estimates of the direct and indirect import contents of a unit of each component of final demand for the three years for which tables were available. The direct import content represents the imports which entered final demand without being processed in the domestic productive sector. (Examples are tourism expenditure abroad by Irish residents and cars manufactured abroad, both of which enter domestic consumption without processing by the domestic pro-ductive sector.) The indirect import content is the imported raw materials embodied in domestically produced goods entering final demand. For the purpose of this study final demand has been disaggregated into a wide range of categories. The results of this analysis are shown in Table 1.3.

Over the period 1964 to 1975 the import content of personal consumption showed the biggest rise. This period coincided with the relaxation of tariff barriers, the Anglo-Irish Free Trade Agreement and Ireland's entry into the EEC in 1973, as well as major structural changes in the economy itself. The rise in the import content of consumption was particularly large in the 1969-75 period, which includes the reduction in barriers to trade consequent on EEC membership. Looking at consumption on a disaggregated basis it is possible to examine the degree to which the rise in import content has

Table 1.3: *Comparison of Total Import Contents of Components of Final Demand in 1964, 1969 and 1975*
(per cent)

Personal Consumption (including export tourism*)	1964	1969	1975
Food	n.a.	26.7	36.4
Alcoholic drink	n.a.	9.0	11.9
Tobacco	n.a.	12.4	17.1
Clothing and footwear	n.a.	45.4	59.7
Fuel	n.a.	29.2	45.1
Petrol	n.a.	38.9	39.6
Durables	n.a.	45.5	57.2
Transport equipment	n.a.	47.4	45.2
Expenditure abroad	n.a.	100.0	100.0
Other goods	n.a.	n.a.	65.0
Other services	n.a.	n.a.	10.5
Other goods and services	n.a.	31.4	32.9
Total	27.7	29.5	34.5
Public Consumption	7.7	8.6	11.1
Investment			
Building	25.5	23.9	26.3
Non-building	73.2	73.6	70.9
Total	53.9	47.9	44.8
Change in Stocks			
Agricultural	n.a.	24.0	21.3
Non-agricultural	n.a.	38.1	73.6
Intervention	n.a.	n.a.	18.2
Total	53.9	36.8	50.1
Exports			
Agricultural	18.6	22.0	19.0
Non-agricultural	44.7	40.0	46.5
Merchandise	29.2	32.3	36.0
Tourism	25.3	n.a.	n.a.
Other services	20.9	33.1	32.1
Total services	24.0	n.a.	n.a.
Total**	25.1	32.4	35.5

*For 1964 Personal Consumption excludes export tourism.
**For 1964 and 1975 total exports exclude export tourism.

occurred due to changes in the composition of consumption rather than through the increase in the import content of each component. Comparable data for consumption for 1964 on a disaggregated basis, are not available. The data in Table 1.3 indicate that there was a substantial increase in the import content of a number of components of consumption and these increases account for a substantial part of the observed increase in the import content of total consumption. The increase in the import content of food is particularly marked. The 1969-75 period straddles the entry of Ireland into the EEC and these data support the hypothesis, though they do not prove, that EEC membership, with the lifting of restrictions on food imports, released a substantial pent-up demand. There was also a very big increase in the import content of clothing and footwear. There was a corresponding decline in the domestic net output content of a unit of clothing and footwear consumption, from about 45 per cent in 1969 to only 30 per cent in 1975. The net result was that by 1975 consumption of clothing and footwear had the highest import content of any component of consumption. A similar pattern is observed in the case of consumption of durables and of fuel. The rise in the import content of consumption of tobacco is mirrored by a decline in the tax content over the same period due to the fact that excise duties on tobacco over the period rose by only 40 per cent whereas consumer prices rose by over 100 per cent (FitzGerald, Keegan, McQuaid and Murphy, 1983). In the case of alcoholic drink, petrol, transport equipment and consumption of other goods and services there was little change in their import content.

There was an increase in the import content of public consumption over each of the two time periods, the increase being largest between 1969 and 1975. However, it was still very small in 1975 compared to most other components of final demand. For investment there was little change in the import content between 1964 and 1975. The import content of non-building investment showed a slight fall in 1975 compared with the observed figures for the 1960s. The measurement of the import content of changes in stocks is likely to show considerable variation from year to year. Ideally one would like to examine the import content of total stocks rather than that of marginal changes. To attempt to minimise problems related to the fall in stocks in 1975, the figures in Murphy (1984) were calculated taking the absolute value of the output of each sector going into the change in stocks. The figures for the import content of changes in non-agricultural stocks show a huge rise between 1969 and 1975. (Comparable data are not readily available for 1964.) However, as described above, these results for stocks are of limited value given the small number of observations, and the inherent instability of this component of final demand.

In the case of total exports there has been a long-run tendency for the import content to rise. This effect is due partly to changes in the composition of exports, in particular to the rise in importance of non-agricultural merchandise exports which already had a high import content at the beginning of the period. However, while the import content of non-agricultural merchandise exports fell between 1964 and 1969, it rose considerably by 1975. (These figures take no account of the repatriation of profits.) With the exception of the rise in the import content of stocks, this was the biggest rise in import content between 1969 and 1975 for any of the components of final demand shown here.

In interpreting the data on import content shown above one must take into account the fact that 1975 was a very abnormal year for the Irish economy. The rise in import prices in the oil crisis of the previous year was still having major repercussions on the economy. Profitability was abnormally low and this may have seriously affected value added in certain sectors of the economy. The agricultural sector was also suffering a recession. Even taking these factors into account, it is clear that the import content of certain components of consumption and of industrial exports rose considerably between 1969 and 1975. The changes in this period were substantially greater than in the period 1964 to 1969.

In addition to the disaggregation by component of final demand discussed above, imports into each sector of the economy in 1975 have been disaggregated into six different categories. Table 1.4 shows the direct and indirect import content of the different components of final demand for 1975 crossclassified by kind of import. Details of the methodology for deriving these data are given in Appendix 1. The results, shown in this table, for the disaggregation of imports are broadly in line with expectations. The component of final demand with the highest content of imports SITC 0 and 1 (agricultural produce) is, not surprisingly, consumption of food. Clothing and footwear consumption has the highest content of imports of raw materials SITC 2 and 4. (This category of raw materials include hides and textile fibres.) The fact that the fuel import content (SITC 3) of consumption of petrol is under 40 per cent is due to the high level of tax on this commodity. Exports of services have a high content of imports of fuel (SITC 3) because of the substantial domestic transport content (e.g., expenditure by tourists on Aer Lingus, B + I, etc.).

Imports of manufactured and semi-manufactured goods (SITC 5-9) form a large part of a unit of consumption of clothing and footwear, durables, transport equipment and other goods. It also accounted for a large part of a unit of expenditure on non-building investment, changes in non-agricultural stocks and non-agricultural exports. On the basis of these data it is clear that in determining the volume of imports, both on an aggregated and a disaggregated basis, account must be taken of any changes in the composition of final demand.

In deciding how best to model the determination of imports an important consideration is the initial destination of imports in the Irish economy. If imports are used as an input into the productive sector then they should be

Table 1.4: *Total Direct and Indirect Import Content of Components of Final Demand*

	Merchandise					Services	Total
	SITC 0-1	SITC 2+4	SITC 3	SITC 5-9	Total	Total	
Personal Consumption							
(including Export Tourism):							
Food	21.8	1.9	3.1	9.2	36.0	0.4	36.4
Alcoholic drink	4.8	0.3	2.2	4.1	11.5	0.4	11.9
Tobacco	9.2	1.2	1.2	5.2	16.8	0.3	17.1
Clothing and footwear	0.7	6.0	1.4	51.3	59.4	0.3	59.7
Fuel	0.0	0.3	39.0	5.6	44.9	0.2	45.1
Petrol	0.0	0.1	38.5	0.9	39.4	0.2	39.6
Durables	0.2	1.6	1.1	53.8	56.7	0.5	57.2
Transport equipment	0.0	0.3	0.9	43.8	45.1	0.2	45.2
Expenditure abroad	0.0	0.0	0.0	0.0	0.0	100.0	100.0
Other goods	0.2	4.8	1.4	58.3	64.7	0.3	65.0
Other services	0.1	0.5	1.8	6.8	9.1	1.3	10.5
Public Consumption:	0.7	0.6	2.0	7.4	10.7	0.4	11.1
Investment:							
Building	0.1	1.9	4.3	19.7	26.0	0.3	26.3
Non-building	0.1	1.3	1.0	68.3	70.7	0.2	70.9
Change in Stocks:							
Agricultural	13.8	0.7	2.6	8.7	25.8	0.1	26.0
Non-agricultural	6.1	5.1	8.8	53.5	73.5	0.1	73.6
Intervention	3.3	0.8	4.3	9.6	18.0	0.2	18.2
Exports:							
Agricultural	4.4	0.9	3.8	9.7	18.8	0.2	19.0
Industrial	3.5	2.3	5.4	35.0	46.2	0.3	46.5
Services (excluding							
tourism)	2.1	0.7	9.3	10.1	22.3	9.8	32.1
Total Final Demand	4.2	1.6	4.5	21.2	31.5	2.4	33.9

modelled jointly with the demand for other factor inputs. If, on the other hand, they enter directly into final demand, in particular into personal consumption, the decision to import should be modelled as part of a consumer demand system. As can be seen from Table 1.5 almost two-thirds of all imports in 1975 underwent some transformation in the productive sector of the economy, the bulk of them in the industrial sector. Less than a quarter entered directly into personal consumption without additional transformation. This would suggest that if a choice has to be made, imports are generally best modelled as an input into the domestic productive sector.

If the import content of each component of final demand were constant

Table 1.5: *The Destination of Imports in the Economy in 1975*

Sector	Percentage
Indirect:	
Agriculture	2.2
Industry	52.5
Services	7.4
Total Indirect:	62.0
Direct:	
Consumption: Personal	23.8
Government	0.0
Investment: Building	0.0
Other	10.4
Stocks: Non-agricultural	2.6
Agricultural	0.4
Exports: Agricultural	0.0
Industrial	0.3
Services	0.5
Total Direct:	38.0

over time, when combined with information on the composition of final demand, the information contained in, for example, the 1975 I-O table would allow one to forecast the volume of imports. The variations actually observed over time, described above, show that the import contents have generally not shown such stability. However, it is still possible to use the information contained in the I-O table to obtain a rough indication of the extent to which the rise in import penetration has been due to a shift in the composition of final demand in favour of goods with a high import content or to a substitution of imports for similar domestically produced goods. Table 1.6 shows both the ratio of total imports to final demand and the ratio of total imports to a weighted average of the components of final demand where all variables are at constant prices; the weights used are the total import contents of each component of final demand taken from the 1975 I-O table. (The two series are scaled to be equal in 1960.)

If all the explanation for the rise in the import penetration of the economy lay with the changing composition of final demand the scaled weighted final demand series would be constant over time. Any increase in this ratio is an indication of the extent to which import penetration has occurred due to a loss of competitiveness by Irish industry on the home market. This loss of competitiveness may have been due to either the dismantling of barriers to trade or to a rise in domestic costs of production compared to those in competing countries. The difference between the growth in the scaled weighted ratio and the unadjusted ratio is an indication of the extent to which the growth in import penetration has occurred due to a change in the composition of final demand arising from changes in domestic tastes. This change in tastes may itself be a reflection of the growth in the standard of living over the period. The results of this analysis suggest that over the period studied, about one-third of the increase in import penetration was due to a change in the composition of final demand and about two-thirds to factors affecting the competitiveness of Irish industry.

Table 1.6: *Total Imports in Volume as a Percentage of Final Demand*

	Weighted	Unweighted
1960	24.9	24.9
1961	26.3	26.7
1962	26.6	27.1
1963	27.5	28.3
1964	29.3	30.5
1965	29.8	31.2
1966	30.4	31.7
1967	30.1	31.5
1968	30.7	33.0
1969	31.5	34.7
1970	31.5	34.5
1971	32.1	34.7
1972	31.4	34.2
1973	33.5	37.2
1974	32.3	35.8
1975	30.6	32.8
1976	32.4	35.5
1977	32.4	36.6
1978	33.7	38.4
1979	35.6	40.9
1980	34.5	39.0
1981	34.6	38.8
1982	33.9	37.5

Source: Department of Finance Databank.

1.4 *Outline of the Rest of the Paper*

The derivation of the "basic" model of import determination from the micro-economic theory of the firm is described in Chapter 2. This basic model, and the related variants which are applied in the rest of the paper to each of the different categories of imports, are described here. In practice it is tailored to reflect the special factors affecting the demand for each category of imports. In addition Chapter 2 describes the model used to determine the volume of imports of tourism services (expenditure by Irish residents abroad). This model is derived as part of a consumer demand system.

The data are described briefly in Chapter 3. A more detailed outline of their origins and derivation is given in a separate technical paper (FitzGerald, 1987).

The determinants of imports are examined at a disaggregated level using a six-way breakdown. Because of problems obtaining consistent data on imports classified by use, the breakdown actually examined is based on the Standard International Trade Classification system. The six categories examined are imports of food and agricultural produce (SITC 0 and 1), raw materials (SITC 2 and 4), energy (SITC 3), other merchandise imports (SITC 5 to 9), tourism imports and other services imports. Chapters 4 to 8 describe the results of applying the model or models of import determination to each category of imports. In Chapter 9 the results from both the analysis of dis-aggregated and aggregated data for imports are described and compared with the results from previous studies. Finally, the conclusions of this study concerning the determinants of Irish imports are set out in Chapter 10 together with the implications they carry for future economic policy.

Chapter 2

MODELS OF IMPORT DETERMINATION

2.1 *Introduction*

There are a number of different possible approaches to modelling the determinants of Irish imports. No one approach stands out as being necessarily superior to all others. To a substantial extent it depends on the nature of the imports and the structure of the economy being examined. In the case of Ireland, because of its small size, a significant proportion of the goods imported are not competing directly against an Irish-made product. In addition, as discussed in the previous chapter, the bulk of imports are used as an input into the domestic productive sector. As Van Bochove (1982) shows, this situation is common to many other countries. As a result, it is most appropriate to model imports as one of a number of inputs into the productive sector. The general model derived from the micro-economic theory of the firm, on which such an approach is based, is outlined in Section 2.2 of this chapter. It differs from the more *ad hoc* approach adopted by many previous studies of imports in Ireland (Leser, 1967; Baker, Durkan and Neary, 1969 and 1970; McAleese, 1970; Kelleher and Sloane, 1976; FitzGerald, 1979a; Boylan *et al.*, 1979; Lynch, 1984 and O'Reilly, 1985).

While the input-output data, discussed in Chapter 1, suggests that one should concentrate on models of demand derivable from production theory, the fact that a significant minority of each SITC category of imports enters directly into final demand should be taken into account in actually implementing the model. This issue, together with the treatment of technical progress and the effects of freeing of trade are also considered in Section 2.2.

The general model is developed on the assumption that firms are free to vary their demand for all factors of production within a single time period. Clearly this is unrealistic in the case of investment and firms may often have to operate at levels of capital stock which differ from their long-run optimum levels. However, if it is assumed that firms attempt to minimise their variable costs in each period conditional on the given levels of the fixed factors, the general model described in Section 2.2 must be modified. This alternative model of the temporary equilibrium behaviour of producers is described in Section 2.3.

The general models described in Sections 2.2 and 2.3 are modified in a number of ways to tailor them to the circumstances appropriate to the different sub-categories of imports which are modelled in Chapters 4 to 8. The changes required to model the demand for energy imports are described in detail in Section 2.4 of this chapter. It also describes the model, derived from consumer theory, which is used to analyse the determinants of imports of tourism services. Section 2.5 considers some of the issues which arise in estimating these models.

2.2 *The General Model*

The production sector of the economy can be described by a transformation function or production possibility set 2.1 where Q' is a vector of outputs and X' is a vector of domestically produced and imported inputs. (Time subscripts are ignored throughout this section.)

$$t(Q',X') = 0 \tag{2.1}$$

This equation shows the sets of input and output bundles which are technically possible. Provided that this transformation function is well behaved[1] there exists a unique joint cost function. Given the vector of input prices P', this joint cost function 2.2 describes the least cost combination of inputs which are required to produce a given set of outputs.

$$C = C(Q', P') \tag{2.2}$$

This cost function will be non-decreasing in input prices; the cost of producing a given set of outputs will not decrease with an increase in input prices (where input prices are strictly positive). The cost function is positively linear homogeneous in input prices; a common percentage change in all input prices will leave the cost minimising bundle of inputs unchanged. It will also be concave in the input prices for a given set of outputs implying a non-increasing marginal rate of substitution between factors. This joint cost function is dual to the transformation function (2.1).

The advantage of working with the cost function is that, when differentiated with respect to the price of each factor, imported or domestic, the resulting equations, 2.3, express the demand for each factor as a function of the prices of all factors, P_j and the given (fixed) set of outputs Q_i (Diewert, 1974).

$$dC/dP_j = X_j = G(Q_1, \ldots, Q_n, P_1, \ldots, P_n) \tag{2.3}$$

---

1. Provided that the transformation function is non-empty and continuous for all combinations of outputs and inputs and that it has input requirement sets satisfying free disposal and convexity from below (McFadden, 1978).

As a result, when the joint cost function is approximated by a flexible functional form the resulting factor demand functions take on a reasonably tractable form. It is this basic model which underlies the empirical work described in the rest of the paper. However, to turn it into a model capable of empirical implementation, a suitable functional form must be specified and some restrictions must be placed on it to make it usable.

The possible range of outputs Q_i and factors of production X_j is almost infinite. To make the model amenable to empirical examination it is necessary to restrict the number of inputs and outputs. This involves either omitting certain variables or aggregating groups of inputs or outputs into aggregate variables which appear in the equation to be estimated. These restrictions involve assumptions concerning the separability of the groups of variables, assumptions which should, if sufficient data are available, be tested rather than imposed.

In a small open economy, such as Ireland, with free trade and freedom of establishment the range of potential outputs and inputs includes those of countries other than Ireland. It is quite possible that, by locating different stages of the production of a good in different countries, labour, capital, and materials from a number of countries may all be used in producing the final product. However, as shown in FitzGerald (1984) and Bradley and Fitz-Gerald (1987), provided that inputs in Ireland are homothetically weakly separable from inputs in all other countries, the conditions for a two-stage optimisation process exist. In this case, firms first decide the country in which to locate production and then decide on the appropriate mix of inputs (including imported inputs) within that country to produce the given output. Thus, if a minimum of homothetic weak separability of Irish inputs from foreign inputs is assumed, the prices of foreign inputs can be excluded from the cost function. The problems which may arise from this restriction may be reduced by the estimation of separate equations for different categories of imports, as discussed below.

Given a limited data sample it is necessary to put further restrictions on the range of domestic inputs and outputs to reduce the number of parameters to be estimated. The most common restriction placed on the joint cost function, 2.2, is the imposition of input-output separability. This restriction implies that all individual outputs can be aggregated into a single output from the productive sector, Q. This also involves the assumption that the joint cost function is homothetic in output. On the assumption of constant returns to scale, together with the restrictions outlined above, the joint cost function can be written as the unit cost function D (2.4).

$$C = Q.D(P_1 , \dots , P_n) \tag{2.4}$$

The resulting factor demand equations for the n factors of production (including imports) are given by Equation 2.5.

$$dC/dP_j = X_j = Q \cdot dD/dP_j \qquad (2.5)$$

or

$$X_j/Q = dD/dP_j \qquad (2.6)$$

That is the share of input i in the volume of total output (2.6) is determined by differentiating the unit cost function with respect to the price of the input.

Even with the imposition of input-output separability there is still a vast range of potential inputs. In this paper it is assumed that the different kinds of capital are homothetically weakly separable from all other inputs so that capital can be treated as a single input. A similar assumption is made concerning labour. In the case of imports this assumption is not imposed. Imports are disaggregated into six different categories and modelled separately and in Chapter 9 informal tests are made to see whether imports too can be treated as an aggregate input. If imports were separable from all other inputs the unit cost function could be rewritten as in 2.7 where P_k, P_1, and P_m are the aggregate price indices for capital, labour and imports. (In the case of Geary

$$C = Q.D(P_k, P_1, P_m) \qquad (2.7)$$

and McDonnell (1980) a fourth input was included, domestic materials.) If imports are separable from all other inputs, the volume of imports can be modelled as a single equation. However, if, in testing, the different categories of imports are found not to be jointly weakly separable from all other inputs, then separate demand functions for each category of imports must be estimated and the unit cost function takes the form 2.8 where P_{m1} to P_{mn} are the prices of the different categories of imports. This was the approach taken by Leser (1967), McAleese (1970), FitzGerald (1979a) and Bradley et al. (1981). The results of applying this approach are described in Chapters 4 to 8.

$$C = Q.D(P_k, P_1, P_{m1}, \dots, P_{mn}) \qquad (2.8)$$

Ideally the disaggregation of imports should be done on the basis of the end use of the imports (e.g., materials for further production, producer capital goods, etc.). However, as discussed in Chapter 3, the data on imports by use are very unsatisfactory. Instead the disaggregation is done on the basis of Standard International Trade Classification (SITC) data. No attempt was made to disaggregate by country of origin. From the point of view of the Irish producer the country of origin of inputs is not important. While the country of origin of imports may be an indication of the type of import, the SITC data probably provide a better basis for such a distinction. Obviously if it were desired to model the behaviour of trade flows between countries a different approach would be called for (see Winters, 1984 and 1985).

The decision on the appropriate functional form for the cost function is affected by the number of different factors in the cost function, the separability assumptions which are to be imposed or to be tested, and the desire to impose a minimum of restrictions on the possible values of the elasticities of substitution between factors. To this end, one of a set of flexible functional forms seems the most appropriate. These forms are generated by taking a Taylor series expansion of the cost function, expanding it around an appropriate value. In the case of this study, the Generalised Leontief functional form is preferred as it generates equations involving the share of factors in the volume of output rather than shares in the value of output. This is desirable since the volume of output is generally forecast with greater reliability in models of the Irish economy and, more importantly, this approach makes possible an *ad hoc* relaxation of the strict assumption of input-output separability. The Generalised Leontief unit cost function is shown in Equation 2.9.

$$C = Q[a_0 + \Sigma a_i P_i^{\frac{1}{2}} + 0.5 . \Sigma \Sigma a_{ij} (P_i.P_j)^{\frac{1}{2}}] \tag{2.9}$$

When the cost function 2.9 is differentiated with respect to the factor prices it generates the demand functions for the different inputs. This formulation has been augmented by the inclusion of factor specific technical progress proxied by a time trend (t) and dummies (D) for shifts in behaviour due to EEC entry or other similar changes in circumstances. Equation 2.10 is the resulting equation for the demand for factor X_i. The significance of the technical progress and dummy variables can be tested by a simple test on the coefficients on these terms.

$$X_i = dC/dP_i = Q[a_i . (1/P_i)^{\frac{1}{2}} + a_{ii} + \underset{i \neq j}{\Sigma \Sigma} a_{ij} . (P_j/P_i)^{\frac{1}{2}} + a_{it} . t + a_{id} . D] \tag{2.10}$$

Homogeneity is imposed by dropping the first order term from the Taylor series expansion, a_i. The imposition of homogeneity means that a common percentage change in all prices, leaving relative prices unchanged, will not change the demand for any input. Homogeneity should, preferably, be tested for rather than imposed in estimation. Because of problems arising from the absence of suitable data, in particular for the price of domestic material inputs, it may be rejected in estimation.

The specification outlined above adopts as a maintained hypothesis the separability of inputs from outputs. As Hall (1973) has shown this implies that the joint cost function, 2.2, can be written in the following form:

$$C = F(Q') . H(P') \tag{2.11}$$

In practice this means that none of the components of final demand (or output) appears as a separate argument in the equations. This also means that the elasticity of demand for each of the factors of production with respect to a change in a component Q_i of final demand or output is identical, i.e.,

$$\delta X_j / \delta Q_i \cdot Q_i / X_j = Q_i / F(Q') \cdot \delta F / \delta Q_i \qquad (2.12)$$

In the standard approach where input-output separability is imposed by treating total output as the sum of its components, the marginal propensity to import out of each component of final demand or output is identical and equal to the average propensity to import out of total final demand or output. However, as discussed in the previous chapter, there is strong evidence for Ireland which suggests that changes in the composition of output, holding total output constant, can have an effect on the demand for imports.

An alternative to this approach would be to base the model on the set of equations derived from the general form of the joint cost function 2.2. In such a model all the components of output would appear as separate arguments in the set of equations determining the demand for the factors of production. This approach was adopted by Burgess (1974a) using US data, and by Kohli (1978) for Canada. However, in the case of this study it would result in a model which had an extremely large number of parameters to be estimated. Given the limited data sample available this model could not be estimated for Ireland. An alternative approach to estimating such a model is to replace output in each factor demand equation by a weighted average of its components F_j where the weights, w_{ij}, are the proportion of each component of output Q_i (or final demand) accounted for by factor X_j, where the proportions are taken from the 1975 input-output table.

If the components of final demand are used rather than the gross output of different sectors entering final demand, the resulting output variable must be seen as a composite good incorporating the output of a number of sectors. The underlying cost function will reflect this as will the parameters of any factor demand equation which is estimated. In this paper a weighted final demand variable is used as models and forecasts for the Irish economy use a greater disaggregation of final demand than of output.

$$W_j = \sum_{i=1}^{m} w_{ij} F_i \qquad (2.13)$$

When Q is replaced in 2.10 by W_j, the weighted average of the components of output using the weights appropriate to factor j, the propensity to import (factor X_j) out of output F_i is equal to the share of imports in total output multiplied by the input-output weight w_{ij} (2.14). (In modelling the demand for another factor, for example labour, an alternative set of weights would be used derived from the input-output table.)

$$dX_j/dF_i = dX_j/dW_j \cdot dW_j/dF_i = X_j/W_j \cdot w_{ij} \qquad (2.14)$$

This approach allows the propensities to import out of each component of output to differ. It was suggested by Leamer and Stern (1979) and was implemented by Sundararajan and Thakur (1976) using Korean data, and Kelleher and Sloane (1976) and FitzGerald (1979a) using Irish data. In employing the additional information gleaned from the 1975 I-O table this approach attempts to relax the assumption of input-output separability. It has a parallel in the use of principal components to reduce the number of exogenous variables in a model. However, the essentially arbitrary nature of these coefficients, which are fixed over time, must be recognised. Their use assumes that the ratio of the import contents of any two components of output (or final demand) remains constant over time. While it is apparent from the data presented in Chapter 1 (and the work of Farley (1978) and Henry (1980)) that this is not the case, it is also clear from these data that the differences in the import contents of the different components is very great. As a result, faced with the alternatives of imposing input-output separability or assuming the constancy of the import contents over time and allowing the import contents of different components of output to differ in a set pattern, the latter is likely to pose a less serious danger of bias. In estimation the choice between these two alternative approaches can be made on the basis of which approach provides the best fit.

An intermediate approach between the general formulation based on the joint cost function (2.2) and the imposition of input-output separability as a maintained hypothesis has been tried. This involves the use of an adjusted weighted output variable which excludes industrial exports. Industrial exports are then entered as a separate variable in the equation. The reason why industrial exports were singled out for this treatment was that the data described in Chapter 1 suggest that this item showed a very big change in import content over the period 1964 to 1975. (A similar treatment of investment in machinery and equipment did not, in practice, make any difference to the results obtained from the more restrictive approach.)

The import Equation 2.10 assumes that all imports are an input into the productive sector. However, as indicated in Chapter 1, a substantial minority of imports goes directly into final demand. To the extent that imports go directly into final demand other factors will affect their volume. If the volume of imports which enters directly into final demand M_d is determined by a vector of relevant variables Z, as shown in Equation 2.15, then the total demand for imports, M, can be written as Equation 2.16. (Henceforth in the notation factor X_j is replaced by M.)

$$M_d = H(Z) \tag{2.15}$$

$$M = H(Z) + W_j [\Sigma a_{ij} (P_j/P_i)^{\frac{1}{2}} + a_i (1/P_i)^{\frac{1}{2}} + a_{it} t + a_{id} D]/2 \tag{2.16}$$

The simplest way to handle this matter would be to include consumption or income together with a time trend as exogenous variables determining the volume of imports entering directly into final demand. The precise specification chosen will depend on the component of imports being modelled. The validity of assuming that all imports can be modelled as inputs into the productive sector can be tested by examining the significance of any parameterisation of the relationship described by Equation 2.15. It should be noted that in Equation 2.16, if an intercept is included as one of the variables, Z, the marginal propensity to import will no longer be equal to the average.

Because this model, derived from the cost function 2.9, consists of a set of interrelated equations determining all the inputs into the domestic productive process it should, as a result, be estimated as a system. It is only when it is estimated as a system that the symmetry conditions implied by the specification can be imposed. However, the consistency of the model is not matched by the availability of consistent data. To overcome this problem some inappropriate series must be used to fill essential gaps. The misspecification involved in the use of these series could well seriously affect the results if the model were estimated as a system using maximum likelihood methods (Johnston, 1972). This suggests the desirability of estimating the equation for imports on a single equation basis.

2.3 Temporary Equilibrium Specification

The specification described in the previous section does not take account of the fact that, because of costs of adjustment, output and the realised demand for factors of production may be adjusted slowly towards their long-run optimal level. In addition, because decisions on the optimal level of output and factor demand take time to implement, they must be made on the basis of expectations concerning the future level of prices and output. There are a number of ways of approaching the problems which give rise to firms operating at a temporary equilibrium which differs from their long-run optimal mix of inputs and outputs (Berndt, Morrison and Watkins, 1981). The general formulation of the cost function as set out in Equation 2.9 can be altered to take this into account if it is assumed that certain factors, such as capital, are fixed in the short term. Firms are then faced with a short-run optimisation problem where they attempt to minimise their costs of producing a given level of output by choosing appropriate levels of the variable factors, such as imports, conditional on the level of the factors which are fixed in the short run. The cost function underlying this short-run optimisation problem is the variable cost function, V, which is homogenous of degree one in output Q (constant returns to scale).

$$V = Q \cdot F(P_1 \ldots P_m, K_{m+1} \ldots K_n) \tag{2.17}$$

There are m variable inputs and n-m fixed inputs. The Ks are the volumes of fixed inputs in each time period. Clearly the Ks will vary over time but what 2.17 means is that in any one time period, their levels cannot be varied by the firm in that time period from the levels determined by past decisions. In the longer run the fixed factors are, of course, assumed to be variable by the firm. As a result, the factor demand equations derived from this variable cost function, in particular the equation for imports, must be seen as short-run demand equations. The resulting demands are conditional on the level of fixed inputs in each period and the given level of output. When the levels of fixed inputs are allowed to vary in the long run, for example, as a result of changes in the prices of the variable inputs, the resulting elasticities will be different from those determined by Equation 2.17. The advantage of this approach is that a full dynamic model is not necessary if interest is centred on the determination of the inputs which are variable in the short term, such as imports. The short-run factor demand equations are obtained from Equation 2.17 by differentiating it with respect to the prices of the variable inputs in the same way that they were obtained from the total cost function 2.8 in the static model (Brown and Christensen, 1981). The resulting equation for import i, M_i, one of the variable inputs, is shown below for the Generalised Leontief functional form.

$$dV/dP_i = M_i = Q_v (\Sigma a_{ij}(P_j/P_i)^{1/2} + \Sigma a_{ik}(K_k/P_i)^{1/2} +$$
$$a_i/P_i^{1/2} + a_{it} \cdot t + a_{id} \cdot D)/2 \tag{2.18}$$

The output or activity variable under these circumstances is the volume of variable inputs, Q_v, rather than the volume of gross output. (If a translog functional form were used the dependent variable in 2.18 would be the value of imports M_i and the activity variable would be total variable cost V.) Brown and Christensen (1981) have shown that if the system of Equation 2.18 is estimated together with the variable cost function 2.17, it is possible to derive the long-run optimal levels of both the fixed and the variable factors from the results. However, as outlined earlier in Section 2.2, data problems together with the need to relax the assumption of input-output separability make joint estimation of Equations 2.17 and 2.18 impractical. Thus, the results derived from estimating Equation 2.18, which describe the short-run determination of import demand, must be located in the context of a wider macroeconomic model if the long-run level of this variable is to be determined. However, by separating the long-run and the short-run determination of imports it is possible to derive a more satisfactory and tractable model than could be obtained if the problems of disequilibrium operation were ignored, as in Section 2.2, or a full disequilibrium model were estimated simultaneously determining all inputs.

This approach assumes that factors of production which are variable in the short run can be readily distinguished from factors of production which take a number of periods to alter. In the case of this study the only fixed factor is assumed to be capital (an exception is the model determining agricultural imports where agricultural employment is also treated as fixed in the short run). This approach assumes that the variable factors themselves are completely flexible in the short run. In the case of the equations for imports described in this paper, tests were carried out on the specification 2.18 by allowing different schemes for actual import demand to adjust with a lag to its optimal level. However, these experiments suggested that imports generally adjust rapidly to their optimal level (the exception is energy imports for which a different specification is tried in Chapter 6). This result is in line with that obtained by O'Reilly (1985) for Ireland using quarterly data, which suggested a rapid speed of adjustment for imports towards their optimal level. Similar results have also been obtained for other countries (Goldstein and Khan, 1985).

The significance of measures of capacity utilisation as a determinant of imports has been established in many previous studies for Ireland and other countries (Khan and Ross, 1977; FitzGerald, 1979a; Thursby and Thursby, 1984). However, in the model described above in Equation 2.18, capacity utilisation does not appear. The explanation for its significance in empirical studies lies in the fact that, while imports may be able to adjust rapidly to changes in prices, they are also affected by the slow speed of adjustment of other factors of production and output and the resulting necessity for disequilibrium operation (or operation at a temporary equilibrium level). For example, if the level of output is above its desired long-run level (capacity utilisation is high) firms may use a higher proportion of imports to meet the demand than if their productive capacity and all levels of fixed inputs were at their optimal level. It may pay not to disappoint customers in the expectation that capacity will be adjusted to meet this demand at a future stage.

The demand for imports may be affected not just by output being above or below its "normal" capacity level, but also by disequilibrium in other factor markets. The explanation given above in terms of output could be reinterpreted in terms of the capital stock. When the desired capital stock is different from the actual capital stock there may be an effect on import demand over and above the effect due to the existing level of the capital stock in Equation 2.18. The possibility that a slow speed of adjustment for one factor could affect the demand for another factor was recognised and modelled by Nadiri and Rosen (1969) in an *ad hoc* way. Another more recent example of such a model is Berndt, Morrison and Watkins (1981). In this paper the effect is incorporated in an *ad hoc* manner by appending an index of capacity utilisation as an additional term to Equation 2.18.

If the set of equations described by 2.18 were estimated as a system it would be necessary to impose a series of restrictions (see Brown and Christensen, 1981). Symmetry involves cross equation constraints requiring estimation of 2.18 as a complete model. In the case of homogeneity the requirements are more complex than in the case of the total cost function 2.9. With the total cost function, to impose homogeneity it was sufficient to impose the restriction that the coefficient on the first order item of the Taylor series expansion was zero. In this case the terms in the fixed factors complicate the situation. To impose homogeneity in the short term (i.e., on the variable factors) the restriction which must be imposed on a single equation basis is:

$$\sum_k a_{ik} + a_i = 0 \qquad (2.19)$$

As was seen earlier, to impose homogeneity in the case of the total cost function a_i must be set to zero. If these two restrictions are imposed simultaneously the result is Equation 2.20.

$$M_i = Q_v [\sum a_{ij}(P_j/P_i)^{\frac{1}{2}} + \sum a_{ik}(K_k/K_n)^{\frac{1}{2}} + a_{it}\, t + a_{id}\, D]/2 \qquad (2.20)$$

However, as in the case of the total cost function it is quite possible that data problems and omitted variables may result in the rejection of homogeneity in estimation. In addition, if the variable factors are not perfectly variable in the short term or the fixed factors are not totally fixed, homogeneity among the variable inputs may be rejected in favour of homogeneity among all inputs. For example if all variable input prices rise by the same amount but the prices of fixed factors remain unchanged there will, in the long run, be a tendency to substitute fixed for variable factors. Under these circumstances, if some of the fixed factors involve different intensities of use of variable factors and if the variable factors are not infinitely variable in the short term, producers may alter their mix of variable inputs in the short term in anticipation of changes in the fixed factors. As a result of these considerations homogeneity is not imposed in estimation. In many cases, it was, in fact, rejected.

As outlined in the previous section, an *ad hoc* relaxation of the input-output separability assumption is tried. This involves replacing the activity variable, Q_v, in Equation 2.18 by the weighted final demand variable W_i, defined in Equation 2.13. When long-run, but not short-run, homogeneity is imposed and the capacity utilisation variable (CAPQ) is included the "basic" model becomes Equation 2.21.

$$M_i = W_i [\Sigma a_{ij} (P_j/P_i)^{\frac{1}{2}} + \Sigma a_{ik} (K_k/P_i)^{\frac{1}{2}} + a_{it} \cdot t + a_{id} \cdot D + a_{ic} \cdot CAPQ]/2 \quad (2.21)$$

As outlined earlier, a slow speed of adjustment, together with costs in adjusting factors to their optimal levels means that firms have to plan for the future on the basis of imperfect knowledge concerning the future values of exogenous variables. As a result, the price arguments in Equation 2.21 should be replaced by the firm's expectations concerning those prices. The process whereby firms form their expectations concerning the future is complex and there are a range of possible ways of modelling it. In this paper one approach tried was to proxy the expected value of each price by the estimate obtained from regressing actual levels on lagged values of the relevant price index and other price indices. However, in the one case where expected prices proved more satisfactory than actual prices, both on an empirical and a theoretical basis (described in Chapter 6), a better proxy proved to be a three year moving average of the relevant price indices. When imports can be varied instantaneously within the year, as proved to be the case for most categories of imports, it is not necessary for firms to use forecast values of exogenous prices in making their decisions. As a result, actual values of exogenous prices generally proved more satisfactory in estimation.

2.4 *Other Models of Import Demand*

The models set out in the last two sections were generally applied to the different categories of imports studied and to total imports. However, in the case of imports of energy a further variation on the basic model derived from production theory was found to give more satisfactory results. The model described in Equation 2.18, while it allows for the fact that producers at any point in time may only be in temporary equilibrium, still assumes that every unit of capital is equivalent to every other unit of capital in its physical productivity. This means that, subject to depreciation, a machine which was put in place ten years ago can be combined with the same volume of other inputs to produce a unit of output as can a machine built today. It also assumes that the proportions in which the other inputs can be combined with a machine of a particular vintage to produce a given output can be varied. This assumption of substitutability between factors, after the capital stock has been fitted, is probably unrealistic in the case of energy imports. (The bulk of Irish energy consumption is derived from imports.) For example, in electricity generation, once a power station has been constructed the possibility of changing fuel or altering the technical efficiency of the plant is very limited. Similarly, once a heating boiler has been installed its technical efficiency is not easily altered. As a result of this special relationship between energy and capital, an alternative model to that described above is required.

As implemented in this paper, the vintage model is only estimated for energy import demand on its own. No account is taken of the possibility of substituting labour for the composite capital-energy input in the long run and no account is taken of the effect on output in the long run of changes in energy prices. The model is derived from that outlined in Helliwell and McCrae (1981) and subsequently implemented in the OECD interlink model.

In the long run output is determined according to the production function 2.22 where the energy imports (E)-capital (K) bundle is weakly separable from the labour input (L).

$$Q^* = F[L^*, g(E^*, K^*)] \qquad (2.22)$$

Starred variables represent the desired or long-run optimal levels of the inputs and the output. The optimal levels of each input are determined by minimising total cost subject to the restriction that output is given and that the production function is a binding constraint. It is assumed that the vintage bundle of capital and energy (K^v) is described by a CES production function. Allowing for factor specific technical progress the resulting equation is shown as 2.23:

$$g(E, K) = K^v = A(dE^{((\sigma-1)/\sigma)} \cdot e^{at} + (1-d)K^{((\sigma-1)/\sigma)}e^{bt})^{((\sigma-1)/\sigma)} \qquad (2.23)$$

where K^v = the bundle of capital and energy
     t = time
     A,a,b,d = parameters, and
     σ = elasticity of substitution between energy and capital.

It is assumed that the firm minimises the cost of a given capital energy bundle, K^v by choosing the optimal mix of energy and capital. The value of K^v is assumed to be determined separately in a second stage of the cost minimisation process. (This two-stage optimisation procedure is conditional on the capital-energy bundle being homothetically weakly separable from the labour input (Denny and Fuss, 1977).) The long-run factor demand equations are determined by setting up the Lagrangian Z, Equation 2.24, and differentiating it with respect to each of the inputs.

$$Z = P_e \cdot E + P_k \cdot K - z[K^v - A(dE^{((\sigma-1)/\sigma)}e^{at} +$$

$$(1-d)K^{((\sigma-1)/\sigma)}e^{bt})^{(\sigma/(\sigma-1))}] \qquad (2.24)$$

where Z = the Lagrange multiplier,
P_e = the price of energy,
P_k = the user cost of capital, and
t = time.

The resulting equations will be equal to zero at the optimum (Equations 2.25 and 2.26).

$$\delta Z/\delta E = P_e - zA[dE^{((\sigma-1)/\sigma)}e^{at} + (1-d)K^{((\sigma-1)/\sigma)}e^{bt}]^{(-1/(\sigma-1))}$$

$$. \, d \, e^{at} E^{(-1/\sigma)} = 0 \qquad (2.25)$$

$$\delta Z/\delta K = P_k - zA[dE^{((\sigma-1)/\sigma)}e^{at} + (1-d)K^{((\sigma-1)/\sigma)}e^{bt}]^{(-1/(\sigma-1))}$$

$$. \, (1-d)e^{bt} K^{(-1/\sigma)} = 0 \qquad (2.26)$$

The desired long-run energy import-capital ratio is obtained as the ratio of Equation 2.25 to 2.26

$$E^*/K^* = (P_k/P_e)^\sigma . (d/(1-d))^\sigma . e^{\sigma(a-b)t} \qquad (2.27)$$

If the firm can only implement this desired ratio when new plant is installed, then the vintage based energy requirement EV_t in the time t is defined in Equation 2.28.

$$EV_t = EV_{t-1}(1-h) + (E^*/K^*) . IN_t \qquad (2.28)$$

where h = the depreciation rate. This is assumed to be constant for all vintages, assuming a geometric depreciation scheme.
IN_t = non-building investment, gross.

The actual demand for energy imports in period t will depend on the utilisation rate of the non-building capital stock CAP,

$$E_t = EV_t (CAP)^j \qquad (2.29)$$

where j is a parameter.
Using Equations 2.27, 2.28 and 2.29 and rearranging terms, the demand for energy in period t is defined in Equation 2.30.

$$E_t = (CAP_t/CAP_{t-1})^j (1-h) E_{t-1} + CAP_t^j . IN_t . (P_{kt}/P_{et})^\sigma$$

$$. (d/(1-d))^\sigma . e^{\sigma(a-b)t} \qquad (2.30)$$

The prices in Equation 2.30 should be some estimate of the prices which are expected to hold for the life of the new investment. The precise expectation formation mechanism used is an empirical question to be determined in Chapter 6.

In modelling the demand for imports of tourism the specification chosen is based on the "Almost Ideal Demand System" (AIDS) developed by Deaton and Muellbauer (1980). This model has been used in studies of other categories of imports by Winters (1984), and of Irish consumption data, by Keegan and Murphy (1983), and Keegan (1984). This model has the advantage that it provides an arbitrary first order approximation to any demand system and there is an implicit underlying utility function so that it satisfies the axioms of consumer choice. Given some limited simplification it is linear in its parameters which reduces estimation problems. In the equations to be estimated the dependent variable is the share of the value of consumption of each commodity in the value of total consumption. In modelling tourism imports this is an advantage where the value of such imports is known with much greater certainty than their volume, due to problems in defining the appropriate deflator.

The derivation of this model follows a very similar approach to that used to derive the import demand functions from the theory of production. In this case the AIDS model can be seen as an approximation to an arbitrary demand system or as derived from a particular cost function:

$$\log C(p,u) = d + \Sigma a_i \log(p_i) + \tfrac{1}{2}\Sigma\Sigma c_{ij}\log(p_i)\log(p_j) + u\Pi\ p_i^{b_i} \qquad (2.31)$$

where C   = the cost function,
     p   = the aggregate price index,
     p_i = the price of good i,
     u   = utility,
     a_i, b_i, c_{ij}, d = parameters.

When this cost function is differentiated with respect to the price of each product it gives rise to the following equations which can be estimated (see Deaton and Muellbauer, 1980).

$$w_i = a_i + \Sigma_j c_{ij}\log(p_j) + b_i\log(x/p) \qquad (2.32)$$

where w_i = the share of the value of consumption of good i in the value of total consumption;
    x = the value of total consumption which is equal to the cost function 2.31.

The implicit aggregate price index is of the form:

$$\log(p) = d + \Sigma a_i\log(p_i) + \tfrac{1}{2}\Sigma\Sigma c_{ij}\log(p_i)\log(p_j) \qquad (2.33)$$

In this study 2.33 is approximated by the price index 2.34.

$$\log(p) = \sum_i w_i \log(p_i) \tag{2.34}$$

which is, in fact, very close to the implicit price deflator for personal consumption. Homogeneity is imposed through the restriction that $\sum_j c_{ij} = 0$. With
the addition of an additive disturbance term, and substituting for p with
Equation 2.34, Equation 2.32 becomes the equation to be estimated. If
symmetry is not imposed on the system of Equations 2.32 then there are no
cross equation restrictions so that ordinary least squares is the maximum likelihood estimator. This allows Equation 2.32 to be estimated for tourism
imports alone without having to estimate equations for all the components
of personal consumption. If symmetry is to be imposed, the system of
Equations, 2.32, for all the components of consumption will have to be
estimated simultaneously using FIML.

2.5 Estimation

As outlined earlier, the different models of import demand are estimated
as single equations rather than as a system. In estimating the basic model,
defined in Equations 2.10 or 2.18, there is a choice between formulating it
in factor share terms or with the absolute value of imports as the dependent
variable. If the dependent variable is the share of imports in total output and
an error term is appended, this implies that firms normally make their decisions
in terms of factor shares. In the case of this study it is felt to be more realistic
to estimate the factor demand equations appending an error term to 2.10 or
2.18 implying that firms normally make their decisions in terms of the volume
of inputs. It also facilitates modification, to take account of the fact that a
minority of imports enter directly into final demand (2.16).

Estimation is generally by means of ordinary least squares. Where the
Durbin-Watson statistic suggests the presence of auto-correlation, adjustment
has been made using the Cochrane Orcutt method. In the case of manufactured
imports and total imports it was felt to be desirable to use an instrumental
variable estimator because of the endogeneity of some of the right hand side
variables used in the equation. This problem was felt to be less severe in the
case of the other components of imports representing, as they do, a small
share of final demand. In the case of energy imports, because the equation to
be estimated was nonlinear in its coefficients, it was necessary to use the non-
linear least squares estimator in the TROLL package (MIT, 1983). The data
sample used for estimation is 1960 to 1982. The end date, 1982, was determined by the availability of data. (Fully consistent data based on later versions
of *National Income and Expenditure* (NIE) were not available at the time
this research was undertaken.)

In examining the results of estimation, the normal battery of statistical tests were carried out. Because of interest in the determination of total imports it was felt to be useful to pay particular attention to the standard error of the equations for each component of imports as it conveys some idea of the likely effects of errors in estimating a component of imports on any estimate of total imports. In addition to the normal significance tests on coefficients a number of tests were carried out to examine the stability and robustness of the results. First, a Chow test was carried out where it was suspected that events, such as the signing of the Anglo-Irish Free Trade Agreement (AIFTA) or EEC entry, might have had an effect on the results. Secondly, other alternative methods of modelling changes in behaviour due to these events were tried (time trends, dummies, etc.).

Extensive use was made of the row deletion techniques described in Belsley, Kuh and Welsch (1980) which allows one to identify whether one observation is exerting undue or abnormal influence on the results. In the case of each equation the maximum value of the DFFITS statistic is quoted as a measure of this influence. (Krasker, Kuh, Welsch (1983) suggest that a value of DFFITS greater than $3(p/n)^{\frac{1}{2}}$ indicates undue influence where p is the number of independent variables and n is the number of observations. In this study this ranges between a value of 1.3 and 1.6.) Where the suggested cut off point was exceeded by observations near the beginning or end of the sample, experiments were carried out to examine the stability of the results by dropping years at the beginning or end of the period.

Given the nature of the specification, the validity of a number of important restrictions on the basic model, such as the imposition of homogeneity, were tested using t tests for the significance of the relevant coefficients. Generally, only one or two equations are presented for each category of imports and the results of tests carried out using other specifications are described in the text. The full results of all the regressions are available from the author.

Apart from the range of statistical tests, described above, it was felt to be important to examine the economic plausibility of the results of the different equations. This is particularly necessary if the equations are to be included in a larger model of the economy. However, even if they are not to find a place in a particular model of the Irish economy, it is important that the results be seen in the context of such models. Answers which may seem plausible in the context of a single equation may turn out to have unacceptable implications when viewed in the context of the structure of the economy as a whole. To this end the implications of each equation for the propensity to import are discussed and the elasticities derived from each equation are examined to see that they have the correct signs, which economic theory would suggest, and have plausible magnitudes. In the case where the economic behaviour implied for a particular category of imports is implausible, this must cast doubt on the estimated equation. These doubts are, where necessary, signalled in the text. (The derivation of the elasticities using the Generalised Leontief production function is described in Appendix 2.)

Chapter 3

THE DATA

3.1 *Introduction*

The data used in this study are generally taken from the Department of Finance databank. The version of the databank used is that based on the *National Income and Expenditure 1982* (NIE82). This is the latest version available on the CCS computer containing fully consistent series for all the required variables. The contents of this databank are described in FitzGerald, Keegan, McQuaid and Murphy (1983) and Murphy (1984). The way in which the data are generated is discussed in FitzGerald and McQuaid (1983). This chapter gives a brief description of how the data used in this study were derived, indicating the published sources used and the major adjustments necessary to provide consistent series over the period 1960 to 1982. Additional details are given in a technical paper (FitzGerald, 1987) for the time series data used and Appendix 1 gives full details of the derivation of the input-output data. Section 3.2 describes the derivation of the National Accounts based time series data. Section 3.3 discusses problems in using the trade statistics and Section 3.4 deals with the input-output data.

3.2 *National Accounts Data*

The data published in *National Income and Expenditure 1982* (NIE82) suffer from two major defects which affect their use for economic research: they cover too short a time period and they are incomplete in their coverage. Both these problems have been rectified in producing the Department of Finance databank. The approach used in generating the consistent time series in that databank is outlined below.

The data in NIE82 for the years 1975 to 1982 must be supplemented by the data in *National Income and Expenditure 1970-1982* to give consistent series spanning the 1970s. Even these data published by the CSO are not fully consistent internally. A major discontinuity still remains in the data published in the National Accounts for services imports (this is discussed in Chapter 8).

Over the years there have been a number of major revisions in definitions in the National Accounts. In particular, prior to 1970, the constant price data are only available at constant 1968 prices. The public authorities data prior to 1974 appear in the National Accounts on a financial year basis rather than a calendar year basis. (The public authorities accounts were changed to a calendar year basis in 1974.) The incomplete coverage of the data in the National Accounts was overcome by supplementing it with data from other sources. In the case of changes in non-agricultural stock changes additional data on changes in EEC intervention stocks (an important component of the total) were used to further disaggregate the published figures. The methods used to deal with these problems are outlined in FitzGerald (1987).

Data on employment in the manufacturing sector on a labour force basis were obtained from the Department of Finance *Review and Outlook*. Data on wages in manufacturing were obtained for the years 1970-1979 from the EEC National Accounts for Ireland (which contain more detailed data than are published in the CSO NIE). For the years 1960-70 and 1979-82 data in the *Census of Industrial Production* (CIP) and the *Quarterly Industrial Inquiry* (QII) were linked to the National Accounts data for the intervening years to provide estimates of the wage bill. The details of the derivation of this series are outlined in FitzGerald and McQuaid (1983) and the Department of Finance databank document. The figures for the capital stock were derived from the data on investment by industrial sector which are published in the UN *National Accounts*. The volume series for gross output was derived from the CIP for years up to 1980 and from the *Monthly Industrial Inquiry* for 1980-82. It was brought to constant 1975 prices using the value of gross output in 1975. Average annual earnings in industry were derived as the ratio of the wage bill (taken from the National Accounts) to the numbers employed in that sector on a labour force basis.

The revenue from protective customs duties was obtained from the *Reports of the Revenue Commissioners*. It was divided by the value of merchandise imports to provide a measure of the effective rate of customs duties. The value and volume of gross agricultural output, the volume of output of crops, and the price of fertiliser were taken from the *Census of Agricultural Production*. The value added in agriculture came from the National Accounts. Further details of these data together with an outline of the methodology used to turn the raw data into consistent time series is given in FitzGerald (1987).

3.3 *Trade Data*

The extension of the National Accounts database to cover a detailed breakdown of trade posed special problems. These arose from problems dealing with the trade of the Shannon Free Airport prior to 1965 and discontinuities in the detailed trade statistics. The trade of the Shannon Free Airport was for many years omitted from the standard trade statistics for Ireland. In the years up to and including 1964, the net surplus of the trade of Shannon Free Airport was included under invisible exports in the balance of payments and the National Accounts whereas it should properly have been treated on a gross flow basis in merchandise trade. As well as the netting of Shannon trade, transport receipts were also included on a net basis in invisible trade prior to 1965. The methodology for adjusting the published data for the years prior to 1965 to a gross flows basis, incorporating Shannon trade, is described in FitzGerald (1987).

For the purpose of this study it is important to disaggregate the merchandise trade statistics into a number of components. There are two problems which arise in this regard: the only data available are on a trade statistics basis (not a balance of payments basis) and there are considerable problems with deflators. In the case of imports the general practice in the past has been to disaggregate trade by use rather than by Standard International Trade Classification (SITC) categories. This approach has obvious attractions, giving a clearcut distinction between imports which should be modelled according to the theory of the firm, and imports, entering directly into final demand, which should be analysed using a model derived from the theory of consumer behaviour. However, the deflators which are available are drawn up on a SITC basis. The old wholesale price indices, which covered trade on a disaggregated basis classified by use, were withdrawn in the mid-1970s due to their wholly unsatisfactory nature. (Their weights were based on trade patterns in 1952.) In addition, while data have been published for the 1960-1982 period breaking imports down by use, these data do not provide a continuous consistent series. There have been frequent undocumented changes in the categories of goods treated as consumer goods, materials for further production and producers' capital goods. These changes have not been signalled by the CSO and it is not possible, on the basis of available data, to create consistent series for the period 1960-1982.

The alternative approach is to break imports down by SITC category and use the relevant unit value indices which are readily available for four SITC groupings. The use of unit value indices is itself unsatisfactory (Goldstein and Khan, 1985). In the case of Ireland they exclude many significant items such as computers. However, they are the only price data available. As a result, for this study, it was decided to disaggregate imports into the following SITC categories for which unit value indices are available: 0, and 1, 2 and 4, 3, 5 to 9. These four groups correspond roughly to imports of agricultural produce, imports of certain raw materials (e.g., textile fibres, timber, hides, etc.), imports of fuel and imports of semi-manufactured and manufactured goods. The data on the value of imports in the first three categories were derived from the trade statistics.

The published trade statistics have undergone a number of major upheavals over the past twenty-five years. There are important breaks in the series at 1962, 1966, 1972 and 1977. While these breaks in each case only affect some of the SITC categories, they do affect the four-way classification described above. Because of problems obtaining comparable data it has not been possible to link the series in a satisfactory manner and the series used in this study still contain some discontinuities. However, the magnitude involved was felt to be sufficiently small not to seriously affect the results. Details of these discontinuities and the way they have been treated in generating the data are given in FitzGerald (1987).

The volume series are obtained by deflating the value series, described above, by the relevant unit value indices to give figures at constant 1975 prices. The volume of imports SITC 5 to 9 was derived as a residual by subtracting the other three categories from the adjusted National Accounts figures. This methodology may tend to concentrate any errors in the residually determined series. However, as imports SITC 5-9 represents the majority of merchandise imports, it is the most suitable category to be so determined. The advantage of this approach is that it ensures consistency with the National Accounts, an essential requirement for modelling the economy as a whole.

In dealing with these data, problems also arise due to smuggling, especially due to smuggling of agricultural produce induced by differences in EEC taxes (Norton, 1984, and FitzGerald et al., 1987). The only adjustment made for this factor is the adjustment for smuggling implicit in the balance of payments adjustment of imports.

In the case of services imports, a continuous series, tourism imports can be generated from the National Accounts. When this series, at current and constant prices, is subtracted from the corresponding series for total services imports, residual series are obtained covering imports of other services. However, the problems which may be built into the series for services imports prior to 1965 by the method of estimating gross transport receipts will be concentrated in the residual, other services, series and may result in quite substantial errors in this relatively small residual item. In addition, there is a serious discontinuity in the series between 1974 and 1975. This arises due to the problems in carrying back recent revisions in balance of payments based on new information which is not available for the earlier period.

In addition to disaggregated data on imports this study requires a disaggregation of export data. The methodology for deriving consistent series for total exports and merchandise and services exports on a balance of payments basis is identical to that already outlined for imports. The methodology for disaggregating services exports into tourism and other services exports is also identical to that for imports. It is only in the disaggregation of merchandise exports that the methodologies differ. In the case of exports, merchandise exports are divided into agricultural and non-agricultural exports. Details of how consistent series for these categories are derived are given in FitzGerald (1987). Details are also given there of the series themselves and the transformations, defined in the language of the TROLL computer programme, used to generate the final series. Fuller details of the generation of these trade data are given in FitzGerald (1979b).

3.4 Data from Input-Output Tables

The three input-output tables prepared by the CSO for 1964, 1969 and 1975 provide an important source of information on the structure of the Irish economy in general, and on the role of imports in particular. While they are merely a set of accounting identities the input-output tables, on certain assumptions, do show where in the economy the imported goods go to, what sectors used a substantial volume of imports and how much of the imports go directly into final demand. The input-output tables are used[2] in this chapter to derive the direct and indirect import contents of each unit of final demand.

Any comparison of the results of the three input-output tables is affected by the differences in assumptions and structure of the different tables. The 1964 and 1969 tables were published in a fairly consistent form by the Irish CSO (CSO, 1970 and CSO, 1978) while the 1975 table, published by the CSO on a different EEC basis (CSO, 1983) must be compared with an alternative version of the 1969 table based on that prepared for the EEC. However, these discrepancies probably make little difference to the actual results (see FitzGerald, 1978). The 1964 I-O table, as published by the CSO, treated only complementary imports as primary inputs. For the purpose of this paper this distinction is felt to be unsatisfactory and all imports are treated as primary inputs. Details of the 1964 table on this basis are given in Henry (1972).

For 1969 the EEC format table, as adjusted by FitzGerald (1978) to treat all imports as primary inputs, is used. For 1975 the EEC format table, as processed by Murphy (1984) to treat all imports as primary inputs, is used. The work carried out by FitzGerald (1978) and Murphy (1984) allows a more detailed disaggregation of the published data to be made for 1969 and 1975. The data for 1975 are stored in the Department of Finance databank. The analysis carried out on the tables is fairly standard in nature and is described in detail in Appendix 1.

2. Assuming that the proportion of each input used by each sector of the economy as defined in the I-O table, is identical for each unit of output.

Chapter 4

RESULTS – IMPORTS OF FOOD, DRINK AND TOBACCO
(SITC 0 AND 1)

4.1 Introduction

In considering the determinants of imports of food[3] into Ireland in the recent past, the single most important factor which must be examined is the impact of EEC entry. Prior to EEC entry in 1973, imports of many food products were severely restricted by means of quotas, embargoes, or very high tariffs. The Anglo-Irish Free Trade Agreement of 1966 did little to alter this situation. However, following entry to the EEC in 1973, Irish restrictions on imports of agricultural produce were abolished in five equal stages beginning in 1973 and culminating in free trade in 1977.[4] Entry into the EEC also had an anticipatory effect on the agricultural sector in the year or two immediately preceding entry, and full adjustment to the new circumstances may have continued for some time after all restrictions were abolished. Separating out the effects of EEC membership from the effects of changes in tastes, changes in relative prices and changes in incomes is, as a result, a difficult task.

Section 4.2 of this chapter analyses the trends in the data over the period 1960 to 1982. This is done at both an aggregate and a disaggregate level. The role of imports in the economy is then examined in Section 4.3 to help in determining the appropriate method of modelling these imports in Section 4.4. Section 4.4 presents the results of estimating a number of equations for food imports. These equations are then used to quantify the determinants of Irish food imports and conclusions are presented in Section 4.5.

4.2 Analysis of Trends in Imports of Food (SITC 0 and 1)

While imports of food only account for one-eighth of total imports (see Table 4.1, Column 1), prior to EEC entry they were more affected by restrictions on trade than most other categories of imports. As such they merit special attention.

---

3. In this chapter imports of food are taken to include drink and tobacco (i.e., SITC 0 and 1) except where it is specifically stated otherwise.
4. After 1977 there were still some remaining taxes or subsidies on trade imposed under the EEC monetary compensatory amounts regulations. These were intended to smooth the effects of rapid changes in exchange rates.

In examining the trends in food imports in this section the first question to be examined is the extent to which imports of food were affected by changes in the composition of final demand, especially of personal consumption, and the extent to which they increased their share of any individual component of final demand. This distinction is of importance from a policy point of view. If imports increase because people want to buy more of goods which are difficult or impossible to produce in Ireland (e.g., avocado pears) then changes in competitiveness and resulting changes in relative prices will be less effective in altering this trend. If, on the other hand, people are buying more of certain imported goods than their domestically produced close substitutes, the trend may be more amenable to change through policies directed at improving competitiveness, broadly defined. The ratio of imports of food to total final demand, shown in Column 2 of Table 4.1 shows the cumulative effect of changes in the composition of final demand and changes in import

Table 4.1: *Imports of Food, Drink and Tobacco (SITC 0 and 1), Volume*

| | Food Imports as a Percentage of: | | |
	Total Imports	Final Demand	Scaled Weighted Final Demand
1960	14.2	3.5	3.5
1961	16.3	4.3	4.5
1962	15.0	4.1	4.3
1963	15.2	4.3	4.7
1964	13.7	4.2	4.6
1965	14.7	4.6	5.2
1966	13.7	4.3	5.0
1967	13.1	4.1	4.9
1968	12.6	4.2	5.0
1969	11.0	3.8	4.8
1970	11.0	3.8	4.8
1971	10.3	3.6	4.6
1972	11.5	4.0	5.1
1973	10.2	3.8	5.0
1974	11.0	3.9	5.1
1975	12.3	4.0	5.5
1976	11.8	4.2	5.9
1977	11.1	4.1	5.7
1978	10.1	3.9	5.7
1979	10.5	4.3	6.5
1980	11.1	4.3	6.5
1981	12.2	4.7	7.0
1982	12.0	4.5	6.6

Source: Department of Finance Databank.

penetration of individual components of final demand. Over the twenty-three year period examined, the ratio showed no strong trend. It tended to fall from a peak in the mid-1960s to a trough in the early 1970s, rising again in the late 1970s and early 1980s. However, the variation in the ratio over time was not very great. On the face of it, this would suggest no major increase in the penetration of the Irish market by this category of imports. However, a very different picture emerges from an examination of the ratio of imports to a weighted final demand variable, where each component of final demand is weighted by its food import content. This weighted final demand measure attempts to take account of the effects of changes in the composition of final demand on imports. Clearly the limited nature of the disaggregation of final demand which was possible, given the available input-output data, leaves the possibility that changes in composition within each component of final demand could have an effect on the volume of imports which is not captured by this measure. As explained in Chapter 1, if the structure of the underlying economy remained fixed as in 1975, imports and all other inputs, accounting for a fixed proportion of each component of final demand, then this weighted final demand measure would be identical to the volume of imports in each year. To the extent that this variable differs from the volume of imports in each year it is an indication of a change in the structure of the economy. As is shown in Column 3 of Table 4.1 the ratio (scaled to be equal to the ratio of imports to unadjusted final demand in 1960) has shown a strong upward tendency over the period. This implies that there was a big increase in imports due to increased penetration of the Irish market.

The difference between the ratio in Column 2, which includes both the compositional and penetration effects, and Column 3, which is crudely purged of the compositional effects, shows the effects of changes in composition on the volume of imports. The result of this crude decomposition is that imports of food seem to have been substantially reduced, below what they would otherwise have been, by changes in the composition of final demand. As income has risen a smaller proportion of consumer expenditure has gone on food than on other commodities, such as cars. This compositional effect has gone a substantial distance towards offsetting the increased import penetration of the Irish food market resulting in the overall trends shown by the ratio in Column 2 of Table 4.1.

From the behaviour of the ratio of food imports to weighted final demand, shown in Column 3 of Table 4.1, it is clear that the big increase in import penetration occurred over the period of the reduction in tariffs, consequent on EEC entry, and the two succeeding years of 1978 and 1979. This is by no means conclusive evidence that the increased import penetration was due to EEC membership, but it is certainly consistent with such a conclusion. The big increase in the ratio in 1979, two years after the elimination of all barriers to imports of food, may be due to a lagged adjustment to the freeing of trade, though alternative explanations cannot be ruled out.

In order to get a clearer picture of where this increase in import penetration has occurred, it is worthwhile looking at trends in the imports of the different categories of food. Problems arise due to the absence of appropriate price deflators below the level of total food, drink and tobacco imports. As a result, the value of imports of each category of food is deflated by the deflator for total food imports. The resulting series are expressed in Table 4.2 as a percentage of the weighted final demand variable where these weights are the food (SITC 0 and 1) import content of each component of final demand. Clearly changes in relative prices within the food category could affect these data and this must be taken into account in interpreting the results.

Of the twelve categories of imports shown in Table 4.2, four account for over 50 per cent of the total in 1982: live animals, cereals and cereal products, vegetables and fruit, and other food products. In the case of imports of live animals the figures may be affected in the early 1980s by the distortionary effects of EEC regulations on trade, resulting in abnormal imports (see Norton, 1984). Even if this is the case, it is clear that the proportion of imports in this particular category fell in the early 1970s and has generally remained below the level recorded in the 1960s. The imports of cereals and cereal products have shown considerable variability over the twenty-three year period. However, the ratio of such imports to weighted final demand has been, on average, significantly higher in the years succeeding EEC entry than in the earlier years examined. Much of the cereals imported are processed into animal feed and should be considered along with the imports of other animal feedstuffs (SITC 08) in Table 4.2. Table 4.3 shows the ratio of animal feed more broadly defined[5] to weighted final demand along with the ratio of imports of breakfast cereals, biscuits and pastry products, and other cereals and cereal products to weighted final demand. The ratio of imports of animal feedstuffs, broadly defined, to weighted final demand in the years after 1973 was, with one exception, greater than in every year before 1973. This suggests that EEC entry had some impact on imports of animal feedstuffs.

Imports of other cereals and cereal products (Column 4, Table 4.3), chiefly wheat and flour, were extremely erratic over time, showing no strong trend and no obvious impact from EEC entry. Imports of both breakfast cereal and of biscuits and pastry products (Columns 2 and 3 of Table 4.3), on the other hand, have shown a strong upward trend in the relatively recent past.

---

5. Defined as imports SITC 08 plus imports of the following cereals: barley, maize and sorghum. Imports of wheat are excluded, though some wheat is used as animal feed.

Table 4.2: Imports of Food as Percentage of Weighted Final Demand, Volume

	Livestock	Meat	Dairy Produce	Fish	Cereals + Produce	Fruit + Veg.	Sugar + Products	Cocoa, Tea etc.	Animal Feed	Other Food	Drink	Tobacco
	SITC00	SITC01	SITC02	SITC03	SITC04	SITC05	SITC06	SITC07	SITC08	SITC09	SITC11	SITC12
1960	13.7	0.5	0.2	1.3	11.6	10.5	1.6	12.6	5.3	0.6	3.2	7.9
1961	24.7	0.3	0.2	1.1	14.7	12.0	2.6	12.8	6.3	1.1	3.7	7.4
1962	13.8	0.3	0.2	1.5	12.8	12.4	2.4	11.6	8.1	1.2	4.1	7.5
1963	17.0	0.3	0.1	1.3	13.6	13.0	4.3	12.6	7.2	1.3	4.5	6.5
1964	17.7	0.4	0.1	1.4	13.7	13.7	4.9	9.7	6.8	1.6	4.5	6.4
1965	15.1	0.4	0.1	1.6	24.4	13.8	2.5	10.5	9.6	2.5	4.6	5.3
1966	10.7	0.3	0.1	1.6	21.9	16.1	3.9	10.5	8.7	2.4	4.3	6.8
1967	14.3	0.3	0.4	1.6	16.5	16.5	3.0	11.3	8.2	2.3	4.2	7.5
1968	14.0	0.2	0.3	1.7	17.0	14.8	2.2	12.1	8.9	2.8	4.6	9.4
1969	15.2	0.2	0.3	1.9	11.7	15.1	2.8	10.9	8.4	3.4	4.3	10.0
1970	17.6	0.3	0.3	1.7	13.1	14.3	2.9	10.7	9.9	3.3	4.5	5.0
1971	11.4	0.3	0.3	1.6	17.1	14.7	4.5	10.0	7.4	3.6	4.3	5.8
1972	13.3	0.3	0.5	1.9	18.3	14.9	5.2	9.4	7.5	4.3	5.6	8.9
1973	13.1	0.6	1.3	1.6	16.8	15.1	3.8	7.4	8.3	4.1	6.3	9.1
1974	6.9	1.0	1.3	1.5	22.8	13.5	6.4	9.0	8.8	4.7	4.5	9.1
1975	6.0	1.7	3.0	1.8	23.9	14.0	10.5	9.1	6.8	5.5	5.2	10.0
1976	6.4	2.1	3.2	2.1	25.4	14.8	10.3	9.5	11.6	5.4	5.5	7.7
1977	10.1	2.1	2.7	2.2	23.3	13.5	6.9	13.0	12.2	5.2	4.7	5.4
1978	11.2	2.4	2.7	2.4	17.2	14.9	6.5	12.2	14.3	5.2	5.7	5.2
1979	15.0	2.6	3.1	2.6	18.9	16.2	7.3	12.2	20.0	5.4	6.6	5.2
1980	10.9	4.5	4.5	3.1	23.3	18.5	8.5	12.9	14.6	5.0	5.8	4.7
1981	16.2	6.7	6.3	3.3	23.9	18.9	7.1	10.5	18.4	5.0	5.6	4.4
1982	15.7	5.9	4.5	3.7	18.9	21.7	7.0	11.2	16.1	5.1	5.5	5.4

Source: CSO Trade Statistics of Ireland.

In the case of breakfast cereal the rise occurred between 1979 and 1982 whereas the rise in imports of biscuits, which is already apparent in the late 1960s, was particularly big in the years after 1973. While the major increase in these two items occurred after EEC entry this does not necessarily mean that this was the cause of the increase in import penetration; loss of competitiveness or changes in tastes for biscuits and pastry products may also have had a role. The pattern of growth of other food products, largely processed food, SITC09 in Table 4.2, also shows a steady upward trend over the period; in this case the bulk of the growth actually occurred before 1973 and it remained fairly stable since that date.

Table 4.3: *Imports of Cereals and Animal Feed as Percentage of Weighted Final Demand, Volume*

	Animal Feed	Breakfast Cereal	Biscuits etc.	Other Cereals
1960	10.5	0.3	0.2	6.0
1961	9.0	0.3	0.3	11.4
1962	13.6	0.2	0.5	6.7
1963	9.9	0.1	0.3	10.6
1964	12.6	0.1	0.4	7.3
1965	20.3	0.1	0.5	13.0
1966	17.1	0.3	0.5	12.7
1967	15.1	0.3	0.8	8.6
1968	15.3	0.3	0.8	9.4
1969	13.6	0.4	1.0	5.0
1970	16.8	0.5	1.1	4.6
1971	17.8	0.5	1.2	4.9
1972	17.1	0.6	1.4	6.7
1973	18.3	0.5	1.3	4.9
1974	19.9	0.5	1.6	9.5
1975	17.5	0.7	2.2	10.3
1976	25.7	0.8	2.7	7.8
1977	25.1	0.7	2.7	7.0
1978	20.3	0.9	3.0	7.5
1979	26.1	1.1	3.8	7.8
1980	20.3	2.7	4.6	10.4
1981	24.1	3.0	4.9	10.2
1982	20.0	3.2	4.5	7.3

Source: CSO *Trade Statistics of Ireland.*

Imports of vegetables and fruit showed some growth in the late 1970s and early 1980s. As the price deflator for consumption of this category of food rose less rapidly than that for consumption of food in general, the use of a common price deflator for all categories of imports may significantly underestimate the volume increase in this category of imports over the 1970s. It is possible to develop an alternative measure of the degree of import penetration of this category of imports assuming that all these imports enter personal consumption directly. Table 4.4 shows the ratio of these imports to personal consumption of fruit and vegetables. As can be seen from the table, there was a very substantial rise in the ratio after 1973. Given that the denominator, personal consumption of fruit and vegetables, includes a substantial distribution margin, the implied increase in penetration of the domestic fruit and vegetable market is very considerable. However, the extent to which this increase is due to a change in tastes in favour of fruit and vegetables, which are difficult or impossible to produce in Ireland, or due to a competitiveness problem for Irish producers, cannot be determined from data at this level of aggregation. However, the data make clear the impact of the EEC on the trade in fruit and vegetables. The removal of restrictions on imports, both through the abolition of customs duties and the elimination of quotas, increased the ability of consumers to satisfy their varied tastes. The effect of EEC entry on this category of imports may not only have occurred through reduced protection for Irish goods; in addition, changes in relative prices within agriculture made production of other products relatively more attractive. As a result, the increase in import penetration may well have involved little or no loss of total agricultural output or income, while, at the same time, benefiting the consumer through lower prices and greater choice. To determine the full impact would require a fully articulated model of the Irish agricultural sector.

Table 4.4: *Imports of Fruit and Vegetables as a Percentage of Consumption of Fruit and Vegetables, Value*

	Percentage
1970	27.5
1971	36.1
1972	36.6
1973	37.3
1974	57.7
1975	52.4
1976	53.6
1977	59.1
1978	45.0
1979	38.9
1980	50.7
1981	50.0
1982	37.7

Sources: CSO *Trade Statistics of Ireland* and EEC National Accounts.

Imports of sugar, confectionary, etc., (SITC 06) showed a substantial increase in the 1970s (see Column 7, Table 4.2). The rise may have begun before entry into the EEC but the biggest increase occurred in 1975 and 1976. Since that date the volume of imports has fallen back, while still remaining above the level of the 1960s. However, as a substantial part of this category of imports is an input into the industrial sector it is not possible from these data to say whether the increase was due to an increase in the share of direct imports of these products into consumption, or whether it was induced by changes in the industrial structure.

4.3 *The Role of Imports of Food in the Economy*

In specifying a model of the determination of imports it is important to have a clear idea of the role of imports in the economy: are they used as an input into the productive sector or do they enter directly into final demand? In the case of imports of food (SITC 0 and 1) their role in the economy is complex. Table 4.5 gives estimates of the proportion of imports SITC 0 and 1 which entered directly or indirectly (through the output of the manufacturing sector) into final demand. In the case of imports entering indirectly they enter first as an input into the productive sector and only enter final demand after transformation into other products in the productive sector. Those imports which enter indirectly into final demand are further broken down according to the sector of the economy into which they first enter as an input.

Table 4.5: *Proportion of Food Imports Used as Inputs in Each Sector in 1975*

	%
Agriculture	1.8
Industry	51.3
Services	2.3
Total Indirect	55.4
Total Direct	44.5

Source: CSO Input-Output Table suitably transformed.

Table 4.5 is derived from the Input-Output table for Ireland for 1975 (CSO, 1983), as transformed by Murphy (1984). As a result, the disaggregation of imports of food shown in Table 4.5 is only exact for the year 1975, the year for which the I-O weights were calculated. For other years the breakdown would only be correct if the underlying structure of the economy remained fixed as it was in 1975. This is clearly unrealistic. The preceding discussion, in Section 4.2, suggests that imports of food entering directly into final demand probably showed a more rapid rise over time than did food imports used as an input into the productive sector. This is borne out by the comparison of the 1969 and 1975 I-O tables. Table 4.6 below shows a breakdown of the SITC 0 and 1 import content of personal consumption of food in 1969 and 1975. (Personal consumption of food accounts for the bulk of food imports entering directly into final demand.) It clearly indicates that imports of food entering directly into food consumption rose rapidly between 1969 and 1975 while imports embodied in domestically produced goods remained static.

Table 4.6: *Distribution of SITC 0 and 1 Import Content of Food Consumption, per cent*

Import Content	1969	1975
	%	
Total	15.9	21.8
Indirect	8.2	9.0
Direct	7.7	12.8

Source: CSO Input-Output Table, suitably transformed.

It is clear that a large proportion of imports of food enter directly into final demand. The vast bulk of the rest of these imports, approximately 50 per cent of total imports of food, enter as an input into the industrial sector of the economy. Very little food imports are used directly as inputs by the agricultural or services sectors. However, a substantial part of the input into the industrial sector is processed by the animal feed industry and used as an input, albeit indirectly, in the agricultural sector. As the value added in that sector of manufacturing industry is extremely small, 17 per cent in 1980 (CSO, 1985), the major determining factor will be the volume of domestic output of food and conditions in the agricultural sector affecting demand for feed. The rest of imports SITC 0 and 1 used as an input in the industrial sector should, preferably, be modelled as a function of industrial output and factor prices in industry, using the type of model described in Chapter 2. For the rest of imports, which enter directly into final demand, they should possibly be estimated in the context of a model of consumer demand.

While it might be desirable to disaggregate the imports SITC 0 and 1 further, so that appropriate models could be used to analyse each component, there are serious problems, adverted to earlier, in finding appropriate price deflators. Preliminary attempts at such a disaggregated approach fell foul of this problem. As a result, one is thrown back on a composite model which takes account of the diversity of factors potentially affecting demand for this category of imports.

4.4 *Models of Imports of Food, Drink and Tobacco*

As is clear from the preceding discussion, the modelling of this category of imports poses special problems. A substantial proportion of food imports enters directly into final demand. There is evidence of a considerable increase in import penetration in this area over the 1970s, partly as a result of EEC entry. However, because the adjustment to free trade took place gradually, the impact on each product differed in its timing. In some cases it was only when all tariffs were removed in 1977 that competition became effective. In other cases it was the abolition of quotas, or other restrictions, which were important. In addition, there may have been a lagged adjustment of the domestic productive sector and of domestic consumers to the changed circumstances. An example of this is the import of breakfast cereals where imports did not show a big increase until 1979. In the case of the agricultural sector the anticipation of EEC entry in 1971 and 1972 led to an increase in prices and may well have been responsible for an increased use of animal feeding stuffs even prior to entry in 1973. As a result, it is not likely to be satisfactory to model the impact of EEC entry with a dummy variable set to 0 prior to 1973 and 1 thereafter (preliminary attempts at using such a dummy proved unsatisfactory). Two other approaches have been tried, one where a dummy variable takes on the value 0 prior to 1971, 1 in 1971, 2 in 1972, incrementing by 1 each year up to 9 in 1979 and remaining at 9 in subsequent years. This assumes a very rigid pattern of adjustment to EEC entry. However, the fact that tariffs were adjusted in five equal instalments from 1973 to 1977 lends certain weight to such an approach. A second method is to use the *ex post* average rate of protective customs duties.[6] This is calculated by dividing total receipts by the value of total merchandise imports. This measure has the disadvantage that, under the terms of the Anglo-Irish Free Trade Agreement, it fell in the late 1960s and early 1970s due to reductions in tariffs on manufactured goods. These tariffs did not affect food imports. In addition, in using an *ex post* measure, no account is taken of tariffs which were prohibitive, as they brought in no revenue. In such cases, where tariffs were initially prohibitive and are then reduced to a level where imports become profitable, revenue will increase with the reduction in tariffs and there will be a rise in the *ex post* measure of the rate of customs duty. However, given the huge diversity of tariffs and restrictions in force at the beginning of the sample period, any attempt to calculate an *ex ante* measure would be extremely difficult. As a result, one is thrown back on the *ex post* measure, and the results obtained using it must be treated with some caution.

6. This excludes the customs duties which were the counterpart to the excise duties on domestic production, e.g., customs duties on imported spirits. It is derived as revenue from total protective customs duties divided by total merchandise imports.

A second complication is the existence of smuggling. Norton (1984) has shown that imports in the early 1980s were probably biased upwards as a result of the profitability of smuggling livestock.[7] Once again this is a difficult factor to capture in the data and the existence of such illegal trade must be borne in mind in assessing the results.

The third problem faced in modelling food imports is the fact that they enter the economy through three different channels. In principle, the factors which affect imports through each of those channels are different and each should be modelled separately. However, even if the imports could be separated into three different categories – imports entering directly into personal consumption, imports destined ultimately as inputs into the agricultural sector, and inputs into the industrial sector – suitable price deflators do not exist to allow each to be modelled separately. The alternative approach which one is forced to adopt is to model the demand for food imports as a whole.

Equation 2.16 in Chapter 2 describes one such composite model. In the case of food imports the first model tried is based on that equation. However, the inclusion of the prices of the different factors of production did not prove satisfactory so that, as implemented here, it assumes a fixed coefficient or Leontief type production function. Equation 4.1 makes the volume of imports of food, drink and tobacco, M01, a function of the demand for this category, represented by final demand weighted by the SITC 0 and 1 import content of each component in 1975, FDWM01 and the domestic supply of agricultural produce, gross agricultural output in volume terms QAGG.

$$M01 = 150.3 + FDWM01\ (2.0 - 20.9RC + .028D) - 3.8QAGG \qquad (4.1)$$
$$\quad\ (2.2) \qquad\qquad\quad (4.6)\ \ (1.5) \quad\ (2.6) \quad\ (3.1)$$

$$\bar{R}^2 = .968 \quad S.E. = 13.9 \quad DW = 1.56 \quad DFFITS = 2.8$$

where M01   = volume of imports SITC 0 and 1, constant 1975 prices, £ million,

FDWM01 = final demand weighted by SITC 0 and 1 import content in 1975,

RC   = rate of customs duty, *ex post*,

D   = dummy, prior to 1971 0, 1971 = 1, 1972 = 2, etc. D = 9 for 1979 and subsequent years.

QAGG   = index of the volume of gross agricultural output, 1975 = 100.

---

7. This trade was exclusively with Northern Ireland.

The fit of this equation is not very good. The standard error of 13.9 must be compared to the value of M01 in 1982 of £369 million. The Durbin Watson statistic is in the indeterminate region and the DFFITS statistic indicates that the result was strongly influenced by one observation, that for 1972. The coefficients, with the exception of that on the customs duty variable, are all significantly different from zero at the 95 per cent level. They have the expected signs, a fall in customs duties raises the volume of imports; the years 1971 to 1979 saw a rise in the propensity to import out of final demand; the negative coefficient on the volume of agricultural output reflects the fact that increased supply of agricultural produce reduces the volume of imports. This equation is basically a reduced form equation for the demand and supply of agricultural produce in Ireland.

Column 1 of Table 4.7 shows the implied propensity to consume out of weighted final demand. It rose steadily in the 1960s due to a decline in customs duties. From 1973 to 1977 it rose more rapidly, reflecting the entry

Table 4.7: *Elasticities and Propensity to Import Based on Equation 4.1*

	Propensity to Import Out of Weighted Final Demand	Elasticity with Respect to Agricultural Output	Percentage Change for a One Percentage Point Change in Customs Duties
1960	1.46	−2.30	−30.29
1961	1.52	−1.87	−24.07
1962	1.51	−1.98	−25.58
1963	1.52	−1.79	−23.88
1964	1.58	−1.78	−24.11
1965	1.57	−1.59	−21.77
1966	1.54	−1.65	−22.64
1967	1.58	−1.74	−23.30
1968	1.61	−1.68	−23.00
1969	1.63	−1.71	−24.33
1970	1.64	−1.72	−24.45
1971	1.69	−1.85	−25.09
1972	1.69	−1.67	−22.73
1973	1.77	−1.64	−23.91
1974	1.80	−1.58	−23.36
1975	1.92	−1.67	−21.42
1976	1.93	−1.45	−20.11
1977	2.00	−1.49	−20.64
1978	2.02	−1.50	−20.92
1979	2.08	−1.25	−18.15
1980	2.07	−1.23	−17.98
1981	2.06	−1.06	−16.54
1982	2.06	−1.14	−17.33

into the EEC, and has stabilised since then. The interpretation of this result is obviously very dependent on the manner in which EEC entry is parameterised and as such, has no rigorous basis. In considering the implications of the result, the coefficient on weighted final demand must be interpreted jointly with the input-output coefficients used in generating the weighted final demand variable. The weighted final demand variable is defined in Equation 4.2.

$$FDWM01 = \Sigma_i w_i F_i \qquad (4.2)$$

where w_i are the intput-output weights,

F_i are the components of final demand, e.g., consumption of food.

As a result $[\delta FDWM01/\delta F_i] = w_i$ from 4.2 and $[\delta M01/\delta FDWM01] = 2.0 - 20.9RC + .028D$ from 4.1. Therefore $[\delta M01/\delta FDWM01] . [\delta FDWM01/\delta F_i] = w_i(2.0 - 20.9RC + 0.28D)$. For 1982 this equation implies a marginal propensity to import out of food consumption of .218 (2.06) = 0.45. This propensity to import is very high for a country which is a major producer of food. The elasticity of imports SITC 0 and 1 with respect to gross agricultural output is shown in Column 2 of Table 4.7. Given the magnitude of the variables, this result implies that a unit of increase in the volume of gross agricultural output will serve to reduce the volume of imports by 0.44 units — a plausible result as so much of our agricultural produce is exported. The percentage change in the volume of imports for a one percentage point change in the *ex post* rate of customs duty is shown in Column 3 of Table 4.7. A one percentage point rise in the *ex post* rate of customs duty in 1960 would have reduced the volume of imports by 30 per cent, whereas the same change in 1982 would have reduced the volume of imports by 17 per cent. However, it must be remembered that the coefficient on which this elasticity is based, is not well defined.

An alternative approach to modelling total imports of food is to develop independent models for the different categories of food imports and amalgamate them in one equation, 4.3, for estimation. (This is the approach adopted in Equation 2.16 in Chapter 2.)

$$M01 = MC + MMAT \qquad (4.3)$$

where MC   = imports of food entering directly into consumption.

MMAT = imports of food used as an input in the domestic productive sector.

For the imports which enter directly or indirectly into the agricultural sector, it is felt to be more appropriate to assume that that sector attempts to maximise profits rather than, as is assumed in the "basic" model of Chapter 2, that firms or farmers treat output as exogenous and minimise costs conditional on that output. Farmers are assumed to choose the optimum level of output, and mix of variable inputs, subject to a vector of the price of output, the prices of variable inputs, and the sector's endownment of capital and labour. The latter are both assumed fixed in the short run. On the basis of this assumption, and on the assumption that the technology is well behaved, it can be represented by a restricted profit function (Diewert, 1974). The details of this approach are similar to those for the "basic" model discussed in Chapter 2. An example of such an approach to modelling imports is Kohli (1978). Choosing a Generalised Leontief functional form for the restricted profit function imposing homogeneity in the short run in variable input prices and homogeneity in fixed inputs (Diewert, 1974), the resulting equation for the demand for imported agricultural goods used as input into the agricultural sector is given by 4.4.

$$MMAT = QAG(b_{11} + b_{12}(PQAGG/PM01)^{\frac{1}{2}} + b_{13}(PF/PM01)^{\frac{1}{2}} +$$
$$c_{11}(KAG/EAG)^{\frac{1}{2}}) \tag{4.4}$$

where QAG = value added in agriculture, constant 1975 prices, £ million,
PQAGG = price of gross agricultural output, 1975 = 1,
PM01 = price of imports SITC 0 and 1, 1975 = 1,
KAG = capital stock in agriculture, constant 1975 prices, £ million,
EAG = employment in agriculture, thousands,
MMAT = volume of imported materials SITC 0 and 1 used in agri-culture which is unknown,
PF = index of price of fertiliser input, 1975 = 100.

An appropriate equation to estimate the volume of imports SITC 0 and 1 entering into food consumption is given in 4.5.

$$MC = a_1 + CFOOD(c_2 + c_3 D) \tag{4.5}$$

where MC = volume of imports SITC 0 and 1 entering consumption (unknown),
CFOOD = personal consumption of food at constant 1975 prices, £ million,
D = dummy, as used in Equation 4.1.

Ideally, there should be a third category of imports, imports entering as an input into the industrial sector, which are not destined to be used indirectly as inputs into the agricultural sectors. However, empirical testing suggested that the inclusion of a model of this additional category did not improve the results. Consequently, these imports are modelled together with the imports entering directly into food consumption.

Putting the models defined in Equations 4.4 and 4.5 together gives the equation eventually estimated, 4.6.

$$M01 = 283.5 + CFOOD(.17 + .01D) + QAG(-1.34 + .20(PQAGG/PM01)^{\frac{1}{2}}$$
$$\quad\;(3.6) \qquad\qquad (1.4)\;\;(2.8) \qquad\qquad (4.3)\;\;\;(1.3)$$

$$\qquad + .02(PF/PM01)^{\frac{1}{2}} + .23(KAG/EAG)^{\frac{1}{2}}) \qquad\qquad\qquad (4.6)$$
$$\qquad\;\;(1.3) \qquad\qquad\quad (2.9)$$

$\overline{R}^2$ = .982   S.E. = 10.54   DW = 2.23   DFFITS = 2.24

where CFOOD = personal consumption of food, at constant 1975 prices, £ million,
PQAGG = index of price of gross agricultural output, 1975 = 1.0,
PM01 = index of price of imports SITC 0 and 1, 1975 = 1.0,
PF = index of price of fertiliser input, 1975 = 100,
EAG = employment in agriculture, thousands,
KAG = capital stock in agriculture, constant 1975 prices, £ million.

This equation shows a somewhat better fit than did Equation 4.1. The Durbin Watson statistic is still in the inconclusive region. The coefficients on the ratio of fixed inputs, capital and labour, and on the dummy variable for EEC entry are significant, as are the intercept and the coefficient on QAG. The coefficients of the two relative price terms are not significant, though the implied elasticities are plausible.

Table 4.8 below sets out the implications of the coefficients for the elasticities of imports with respect to the key exogenous variables.

The effect of a unit change in net agricultural output ($\delta M01/\delta QAG$), shown in Column 1, is to reduce the volume of imports by between 0.59 units in 1960 and 0.21 units in 1982. These results are consistent with those obtained from Equation 4.1. The fall in the supply effect over time is not surprising and indicates the increased specialisation of Irish agricultural output and the increasing diversity of consumer demands. Today the bulk of any change in agricultural output finds its way onto foreign markets.

The marginal propensity to import out of a change in food consumption ($\delta M01/\delta CFOOD$) is shown in Column 2. It rose from 0.17 in the 1960s to 0.27 in the 1980s. Obviously the pattern which this change took in the 1970s is heavily dependent on the nature of the dummy variable used for EEC entry. None the less, it is clear that there was a substantial increase in the penetration of the Irish food market as a result of the freeing of trade. This propensity to import includes both the direct effect on food imports and the indirect effects on imports which are used as inputs in the industrial sector. Ignoring the impact on imports used as inputs into the agricultural sector,

Table 4.8: Elasticities and Propensity to Import Based on Equation 4.6

	Propensity to Import Out of:		Elasticity with Respect to:			
	Agricultural Output	Food Consumption	Agricultural Output Prices	Own Price	Fertiliser Prices	Capital Stock
1960	-.59	.17	.36	-.68	.32	.76
1961	-.58	.17	.29	-.53	.25	.61
1962	-.58	.17	.30	-.55	.26	.65
1963	-.57	.17	.26	-.49	.22	.59
1964	-.55	.17	.27	-.49	.23	.60
1965	-.53	.17	.23	-.43	.20	.53
1966	-.52	.17	.24	-.45	.21	.56
1967	-.51	.17	.26	-.47	.22	.60
1968	-.49	.17	.25	-.45	.21	.60
1969	-.48	.17	.24	-.45	.21	.61
1970	-.46	.17	.25	-.45	.20	.64
1971	-.44	.18	.26	-.48	.22	.71
1972	-.41	.19	.26	-.47	.21	.67
1973	-.40	.20	.25	-.44	.19	.65
1974	-.39	.22	.23	-.44	.21	.68
1975	-.35	.23	.26	-.53	.26	.76
1976	-.34	.24	.22	-.42	.20	.64
1977	-.34	.25	.22	-.41	.19	.68
1978	-.31	.26	.22	-.40	.19	.67
1979	-.28	.27	.16	-.30	.14	.52
1980	-.26	.27	.16	-.31	.15	.58
1981	-.23	.27	.13	-.26	.12	.50
1982	-.21	.27	.16	-.30	.14	.58

this propensity to import out of food consumption can be roughly compared to the average total SITC 0 and 1 import content of food consumption in 1969 and 1975. For 1969 the I-O based import content was 15.9 per cent compared to the marginal propensity to import of 17.4 and in 1975 the I-O content was 21.8 compared to a propensity of 22.6. While these figures have very different bases, and are not strictly comparable, they are mutually consistent. This propensity to import, out of food consumption, while not strictly comparable to that obtained from Equation 4.1, is significantly smaller than it, and seems on the whole the more plausible, given the fact that Ireland is a major food producer. For the reasons given above the results from Equation 4.6 are more plausible than those from Equation 4.1.

The elasticity of imports with respect to output prices ($\delta \log M01/\delta \log$ PQAGG) is shown in Column 3 of Table 4.8. It shows the expected positive sign. Increased profitability in agriculture induces increased output which, in turn, requires more of the variable input-imports of animal feed. This elasticity is not very large and is not significantly different from zero. Column 4 shows the own price elasticity of SITC 0 and 1 imports. It is, as expected, negative and is substantially larger than the output price elasticity. This reflects the fact that the elasticity with respect to fertiliser prices (Column 5) is positive indicating that fertiliser and imported feed are substitutes. However, this latter elasticity is not significantly different from zero.

The elasticity with respect to changes in the capital stock ($\delta \log M01/\delta \log KAG$) is shown in Column 6 of Table 4.8. It is significantly positive. (The elasticity with respect to labour is identical to that for capital, with the sign reversed.) Increases in the capital intensity of Irish agriculture result in an increase in demand for imported feedstuffs. This is a highly plausible result, as increased capital intensity is generally associated with more intensive methods of farming.

Attempts to parameterise the propensity to import out of food consumption, on the lines of the "basic" model of Chapter 2, to take account of the fact that a substantial proportion of the imports entering into it originated as inputs into the industrial sector, proved unsatisfactory. Attempts to disaggregate imports SITC 0 and 1 into separate food, drink and tobacco categories produced very unsatisfactory results. It was clear that the absence of suitable deflators for each of these categories made such an approach impossible.

4.5 Conclusion

The results of the analysis described in this chapter indicate that entry into the EEC had a big effect on the volume of imports of goods in SITC categories 0 and 1. Leaving aside the supply effects of EEC entry, Equation 4.1 would suggest that the volume of imports of food in 1982 was 50 per cent

Chapter 5

RESULTS – IMPORTS OF RAW MATERIALS (SITC 2 AND 4)

5.1 Introduction

Imports of raw materials (SITC 2 and 4) consist of a miscellaneous grouping of materials ranging from timber to textile fibres and from non-mineral oils and fats to metal ores. They account for a relatively small part of total imports and are used in a fairly restricted range of sectors of the economy. As a result, a major question which arises in any attempt to model them is whether such an aggregate as raw materials imports is a meaningful economic concept. This chapter considers this question and, to the extent that the answer is positive, analyses the determinants of the demand for this aggregate.

Section 5.2 of this chapter discusses the trends in this category of imports over the past twenty-three years and Section 5.3 examines the role of imports of raw materials in the Irish economy. A model of the demand for this category of imports is discussed in Section 5.4 and conclusions are presented in Section 5.5.

5.2 Analysis of Trends in Imports of Raw Materials

Over the twenty-three years 1960 to 1982, imports of goods categories SITC 2 and 4, henceforward referred to as raw materials imports, fell rapidly as a proportion of total imports. Table 5.1, Column 1, shows that while they accounted for over 8 per cent of imports in 1960, they only accounted for 3.5 per cent of total imports in 1982. When expressed as a percentage of final demand, in Column 2 of Table 5.1, there was a similar substantial fall over the period. In considering why this fall took place as with the other categories of imports, the first possibility examined is that there was a fall due to a change in the structure of final demand. Column 3 of Table 5.1 shows the ratio of raw materials imports to a scaled weighted final demand variable in which each component of final demand is weighted by its raw material import content in 1975. The movements in the ratio of imports to weighted final demand should, in theory, be purged of the effect of changes in composition of final demand.[9] The difference between movements in this series and the

9. Clearly the extent to which this is true depends on the degree of disaggregation of final demand undertaken.

Table 5.1: *Imports of Raw Materials (SITC 2 and 4)*

	Raw Materials Imports as a Percentage of:		
	Total Imports	*Final Demand*	*Scaled Weighted Final Demand*
1960	8.3	2.1	2.1
1961	7.4	2.0	2.0
1962	7.4	2.0	2.1
1963	7.3	2.1	2.1
1964	6.8	2.1	2.1
1965	6.2	1.9	1.9
1966	6.1	1.9	2.0
1967	6.3	2.0	2.0
1968	6.6	2.2	2.1
1969	5.9	2.1	2.0
1970	5.9	2.0	1.9
1971	5.8	2.0	2.0
1972	5.9	2.0	1.9
1973	6.0	2.2	2.2
1974	6.0	2.1	2.0
1975	4.3	1.4	1.4
1976	4.9	1.7	1.7
1977	4.1	1.5	1.4
1978	3.7	1.4	1.4
1979	3.8	1.5	1.5
1980	3.6	1.4	1.3
1981	3.7	1.4	1.4
1982	3.5	1.3	1.3

Sources: CSO *Trade Statistics of Ireland* and Department of Finance Databank.

ratio of imports to unweighted final demand is then a crude measure of the effects of change in composition on the volume of imports. As can be seen from Table 5.1, using this approach in the case of imports of raw materials, changes in the composition of final demand had no effect on their volume. To the extent that this methodology is appropriate, the bulk of the explanation for the fall in the ratio of such imports to final demand lies with changes in the structure of the economy due to changes in relative prices of factor inputs or technical progress. However, given the very specialised nature of some of these imports, and the limited level of disaggregation used in generating the weighted final demand variable, it is possible that shifts in the composition of some of the components of final demand might still explain some of the change in the ratio in Column 2 over the twenty-three years.

A better idea of developments in this category of imports can be obtained by looking at movements in each sub-category over the period. In Table 5.2

Table 5.2: Imports of Raw Materials Classified by Commodity as a Percentage of Weighted Final Demand, Volume

	Hides SITC21	Oil Seed SITC22	Rubber SITC23	Wood SITC24	Pulp SITC25	Textile Fibres SITC26	Crude Fertiliser SITC27	Metal Ore SITC28	Crude Veg.Mat. SITC29	Crude Oil – Animal SITC41	Crude Oil-Veg. SITC42	Process. Oil-Veg. + Animal SITC43
1960	1.8	3.4	9.2	26.7	12.4	50.8	13.3	0.1	8.2	2.3	6.5	1.0
1961	2.9	3.9	8.3	25.8	10.5	44.7	14.8	0.1	9.2	2.5	5.4	1.0
1962	3.7	3.1	7.9	26.5	8.8	47.9	15.9	0.1	10.3	2.1	5.5	1.1
1963	3.7	4.4	7.6	31.0	10.7	45.4	17.6	0.2	7.5	1.0	4.9	2.3
1964	3.4	3.4	6.9	31.8	9.7	48.1	16.9	0.7	6.1	1.6	6.1	2.1
1965	3.2	3.3	7.2	34.1	7.6	37.6	16.7	0.4	6.2	1.4	5.7	2.8
1966	3.7	4.6	6.2	27.6	6.1	42.4	21.8	0.5	5.2	1.3	6.1	2.7
1967	2.3	3.5	5.7	31.2	7.7	39.1	24.3	0.5	5.4	0.7	5.1	2.3
1968	2.8	3.3	6.0	36.9	9.1	39.0	25.1	0.8	4.9	0.9	5.9	2.2
1969	4.3	3.3	4.9	34.1	8.4	35.2	22.3	0.7	4.9	1.2	5.6	1.7
1970	3.2	3.0	6.9	31.3	9.8	34.2	20.7	0.5	4.8	2.0	7.1	2.6
1971	2.6	2.5	6.3	38.4	7.4	30.5	20.5	0.6	5.5	2.2	7.7	2.4
1972	5.3	2.8	5.5	37.7	8.1	32.7	15.1	0.9	6.5	2.4	7.7	1.3
1973	5.3	11.0	5.8	39.3	7.3	37.8	14.6	2.4	6.1	2.5	7.3	0.7
1974	2.7	2.4	7.0	42.8	6.0	30.3	20.5	2.6	5.1	1.7	7.6	2.8
1975	1.9	0.9	5.7	25.2	5.7	21.4	14.7	1.6	4.1	1.4	7.9	1.5
1976	2.7	1.5	8.0	31.0	5.6	32.4	12.7	1.0	4.9	1.1	8.2	2.1
1977	2.7	2.5	7.1	24.7	3.9	25.4	9.3	1.5	4.4	2.1	7.7	2.1
1978	2.4	2.4	5.7	27.1	3.4	20.0	9.8	1.6	5.3	1.4	7.2	2.1
1979	3.0	2.2	6.1	30.4	3.5	19.9	9.1	1.7	6.1	1.4	8.1	2.7
1980	1.8	0.8	6.1	26.1	3.8	19.8	9.5	1.5	6.0	1.1	7.3	2.7
1981	1.7	1.0	5.3	26.4	4.3	21.1	8.4	1.8	7.9	1.4	7.8	2.3
1982	0.8	1.1	5.2	21.6	1.3	18.9	9.5	3.0	9.0	1.2	7.7	2.7

Source: CSO Trade Statistics of Ireland.

raw materials imports are disaggregated into 12 sub-categories defined at the two digit SITC level. Table 5.2 shows the volume of each sub-category of raw materials imports as a percentage of the weighted final demand variable for total raw materials imports which gives an indication of the changing importance of each sub-category in the economy as a whole.

Of the 12 sub-categories, 4, wood and timber (SITC 24), textile fibres (SITC 26), crude fertilisers (SITC 27) and crude vegetable materials (SITC 29) account for almost three-quarters of the total raw materials imports over the period 1960 to 1982. In 1983 there was a major change with a big increase in the share of the total accounted for by metal ores. This latter development was due to the opening of the Alcan plant processing alumina in Co. Limerick.

When examined against the background of the weighted final demand variable, the movements in the sub-categories give an indication of their changing role in the economy over the period. Imports of timber and wood grew over the 1960s and early 1970s as a percentage of weighted final demand reaching a peak in 1974. Since then, they have fallen back to the level of the early 1960s. Imports of textile fibres which were by far the largest component of raw materials imports in 1960, measured against the weighted final demand benchmark, fell throughout the period. Particularly large falls occurred in 1965 and 1975. Imports of crude fertilisers rose to a peak in 1968, falling back to a low point at the end of the sample period. The decline was especially significant in the second half of the 1970s. Thus, while 3 of the largest sub-categories of raw materials imports all fell as a proportion of final demand over the period, the timing of the falls was different in each case and the cause of these changes would appear to be unrelated. In the case of metal ore imports, recent developments since 1983 have clearly shown a very different trend which will continue into the future.

5.3 *The Role of Raw Materials Imports in the Economy*

As can be seen from Table 5.3, over two-thirds of raw materials imports were used as inputs into the productive sector of the economy. Clearly a substantial part of the textile fibre imports are used as an input into the domestic textile industry while much of the remainder enters consumption directly. In the case of timber and wood imports, the bulk of them enter either the wood and furniture sector or the building sector. Part of the timber used as an input in the timber and furniture sector will find its way indirectly into the building sector. The demand for these 2 important sub-categories of raw materials imports — textile fibres and timber is, thus, closely bound up with factors affecting the domestic textile and building industries. In the case of the recent increase in metal ore imports, the demand for them will be intimately related to the future of alumina processing in Ireland,

Table 5.3: *Breakdown of Destination of Imported Raw Materials in 1975*
(per cent of total)

		1975
Agriculture:	Total	2.5
Industry:	Total	61.7
of which:	Other mineral products	1.5
	Chemicals	5.8
	Meat processing	1.4
	Other foods	10.0
	Tobacco	1.8
	Textiles and clothing	10.6
	Timber and furniture	9.9
	Paper and printing	2.8
	Rubber and plastics	3.0
	Building	9.3
Services:	Total	5.2
of which:	Non-market health	1.7
Total Indirect:		69.4
Direct of which:	Consumption food	4.8
	Consumption clothing and footwear	12.3
	Consumption other goods	6.3
	Investment — non-building	2.6
	Change in non-agricultural stocks	4.1
Total Direct:		30.6

Source: Reprocessed 1975 input-output table for Ireland (Murphy, 1984).

currently carried out by one firm. As a result, this category of imports is more closely related to the development of a limited number of sub-sectors of the economy than is the case for the other categories of merchandise imports considered in this paper.

Table 5.4 shows the direct and total raw materials import content of certain components of final demand derived from the 1969 and 1975 input-output tables. These results highlight a number of the points made above. For consumption of clothing and footwear, the proportion of raw materials imports which enter directly into consumption has risen over the period while the indirect import content (imports used in domestic manufacture of textiles for home consumption) fell. This is a reflection of the general decline which occurred over the period examined in the domestic clothing and textile industries. The raw materials import content of investment in buildings almost halved between 1969 and 1975, partly due to technical change in the industry, a change that is consistent with the trends in timber imports observed in Table 5.2. In the case of agricultural exports the raw materials import content also fell significantly between 1969 and 1975. This is in line with the decline over the period in the imports of crude fertilisers.

Table 5.4: *Raw Materials Import Content of Certain Components of Final Demand, per cent*

	Inputs Direct Into Final Demand		Total Import Content of Final Demand	
	1969	*1975*	*1969*	*1975*
Consumption of clothing and footwear	2.0	4.6	4.1	6.0
Investment in building	–	–	3.7	1.9
Agricultural exports	0.6	–	2.2	0.9
Total final demand	0.9	0.5	1.9	1.6

Sources: Reprocessed 1975 input-output table for Ireland (Murphy, 1984); Reprocessed 1969 input-output table for Ireland (FitzGerald, 1978).

5.4 *Model of Imports of Raw Materials*

As is highlighted in the preceding section, there was a wide range of forces affecting imports of raw materials over the period 1960 to 1982. While the bulk of these imports were used as an input into the productive sector of the economy, the limited range of industrial sub-sectors involved and their divergent experiences over the period makes any model of the behaviour of aggregate raw materials imports problematic. However, given the nature of this study and the data limitations, due to the absence of suitable price deflators, the necessary separability assumptions are maintained to allow them to be treated as an aggregate and modelled as described below.

Using the "basic" models of Chapter 2, derived from production theory, all attempts to allow for substitution possibilities between raw materials imports and other factors of production proved unsatisfactory. Generally the own price elasticity of raw materials imports was either positive (the opposite of what might have been expected) or not significantly different from zero. While the fits of such equations were generally superior to those obtained from simpler specifications, these results were clearly unacceptable having incorrectly signed coefficients. As a result, an alternative, simpler, specification was chosen. Demand for raw materials imports is made a function of two activity variables: investment in residential building, which could be expected to drive timber and other imports related to the building industry, and a weighted final demand variable, which excludes residential building investment. While the activity variable used should be sectoral output, the variety of sectors involved as consumers of raw materials makes this impractical. Instead the weighted final demand variable is used representing, as it does, a suitably weighted average of the outputs of the different sectors. In the case of the weighted final demand variable the relationship between it and imports is parameterised by the capital stock in manufacturing industry. This allows for the fact that the development of the industrial sector (and capital stock) has involved a shift in production to sectors which use little imported raw materials. The relationship between imports and residential investment is allowed to shift between 1974 and 1975 to take account of the shift in timber imports shown up in Table 5.2 which occurred at that time. The resulting equation, 5.1, is shown below:

$$M24 = 2.394 + FDWM24\ (1.163 - 0.000167KIM) +$$
$$(0.3) \qquad\qquad (4.7) \quad (2.6)$$

$$IRB\ (0.148 - 0.118D) \qquad\qquad\qquad (5.1)$$
$$(3.5) \quad (8.1)$$

$$\overline{R}^2 = .974 \quad S.E. = 4.68 \quad DW = 2.43 \quad rho = -0.434 \quad DFFITS = 1.55$$
$$(2.2)$$

where M24   = imports of raw materials, SITC 2 and 4, £ million, 1975 prices,

FDWM24 = final demand weighted by raw materials import content, £ million, 1975 prices (excluding residential investment),

IRB   = residential investment, £ million, 1975 prices,

KIM   = capital stock in manufacturing, £ million, 1975 prices,

D   = dummy variable, 0 up to and including 1974, 1 thereafter.

The fit of this equation is not as satisfactory as that for imports of food, discussed in Chapter 4. However, all the coefficients, barring the intercept, are significantly different from zero. The inclusion of the dummy variable for the shift in the propensity to import out of residential investment is highly significant. The coefficient on the capital stock in manufacturing is negative, consistent with the fact that the changes in the industrial structure have tended to reduce the demand for raw materials imports. With the freeing of trade in the 1960s the firms producing for the domestic market using imported raw materials have been replaced by firms producing for export which are more capital intensive.

The propensity to import raw materials out of weighted final demand and the propensity to import out of residential investment, implied by Equation 5.1, are shown in Table 5.5. The propensity to import out of weighted final demand fell consistently over the period, due to the rise in the capital stock, from a high of 1.09 in 1960 to a low of 0.80 in 1982. This means that the propensity to import out of, for example, personal consumption of clothing in 1960 was 1.09 times the average propensity derived from the 1975 input-output table (e.g., $1.09 \times .060 = 0.065$). In the case of residential investment the propensity fell from 0.15 in 1974 to 0.03 in 1975. The magnitude of the pre-1975 propensity seems implausibly large and the unsatisfactory nature of the discontinuity must be recognised. However, the propensity for 1975 and later years is of plausible magnitude.

Table 5.5: *Propensities to Import Derived from Equation 5.1*

	Propensity to Import out of:	
	Weighted Final Demand	Investment in Residential Buildings
1960	1.090	0.148
1961	1.086	0.148
1962	1.079	0.148
1963	1.073	0.148
1964	1.066	0.148
1965	1.059	0.148
1966	1.051	0.148
1967	1.045	0.148
1968	1.035	0.148
1969	1.023	0.148
1970	1.011	0.148
1971	0.999	0.148
1972	0.984	0.148
1973	0.971	0.148
1974	0.959	0.148
1975	0.942	0.030
1976	0.925	0.030
1977	0.910	0.030
1978	0.888	0.030
1979	0.861	0.030
1980	0.838	0.030
1981	0.817	0.030
1982	0.800	0.030

The absence of a clear explanation of the shift in the propensity to import out of residential investment is unsatisfactory. While the inclusion of the post-1974 dummy variable helps to improve the fit of the equation on statistical grounds, it does not explain them. Similarly the inclusion of the capital stock as a measure of the changes in the structure of the economy is very much a second best solution. As formulated here, the continuous rise in the capital stock in the future would lead to an indefinite decline in the propensity to import out of final demand resulting, eventually, in a negative propensity. This is clearly not acceptable. There is some limit to the decline in the propensity, though the data failed to yield a satisfactory estimate of where it lies. In addition, this equation could not hope to track the effects on raw materials imports of the commencement of alumina processing.

5.5 Conclusion

In the future, as in the past, trends in raw materials imports will depend on developments in a limited number of sub-sectors of the Irish economy. The results presented above indicate that a satisfactory model of the determination of raw materials imports would involve modelling individually a number of sub-sectors of the economy. In the absence of such a model any aggregate approach to the determinants of these imports must be unsatisfactory. The results described in this chapter indicate that over the twenty-three year period examined, the structure of the economy changed so as to reduce the propensity to import raw materials. For the future, changes, such as the commencement of alumina processing, may reverse this trend. The uncertainty concerning the determinants of this category of imports, when treated as an aggregate, stems from its small size and the limited range of industries in which it is used. However, its small size means that failure to model its determinants in a fully satisfactory fashion need not seriously affect our understanding of the behaviour of total imports.

Chapter 6

RESULTS – IMPORTS OF ENERGY (SITC 3)

6.1 Introduction

Energy imports accounted for upwards of three-quarters of total domestic energy consumption over the period 1960-1982. This means that in modelling energy imports one is effectively modelling total domestic energy demand. As a result, this chapter examines jointly the demand for total primary energy and the demand for energy imports. The domestic supply of primary energy is treated as exogenous.

The energy sector of the world economy underwent a major buffeting in the 1970s with two major oil crises in 1974/74 and 1979 and the resulting huge rise in the price of energy relative to other goods and services. The Irish economy, with its heavy dependence on imported energy, especially imported oil, was severely affected by these events. (In 1973 over 85 per cent of energy imports were accounted for by oil.) The income effect, both directly through the terms of trade, and indirectly through its effects on the growth of the world economy was severe. However, adjustment to these effects was completed reasonably rapidly. Of much longer-lasting significance was the sustained change in the relative price of energy. There is ample evidence that for Ireland, as well as for the rest of the world, the effects of this change have still, many years after it first occurred, not fully worked themselves out. Thus, any examination of the determinants of Irish energy imports (SITC 3) must take account of the magnitude of the changes in the relative price of energy as well as of the extensive lags in the adjustment of the Irish economy to the changed circumstances.

To date the analysis of energy demand in Ireland has been generally based on rather crude or simplistic models relating energy demand to GNP, taking no account of the effects of changes in relative price or of the interaction between the structure of the economy and energy demand. One exception to this pattern is a study by Scott (1980). This allowed for adjustment lags and incorporated price variables into the demand equation. A symptom of this apparent disbelief in the significance of changing energy prices has been the failure to collect and include proper data on Irish energy prices in official publications. In spite of the work by Scott (1980) and the very extensive

71

literature, in particular in the US, on the determination of energy demand, it is disturbing to read in the *Report of the Inquiry into Electricity Prices* (Department of Energy, 1984), that while "it would seem advisable for forecasting purposes to take this factor [price] into account . . . the ESB has decided not to do so".

In this chapter, while the focus of interest is primarily on the volume of energy imports, models are described and estimated which allow some estimate to be made of the elasticity of demand for energy in Ireland with respect to its own price. Section 6.2 of this chapter examines the trend in energy imports over the period 1960 to 1982. Section 6.3 discusses the role of energy imports in the Irish economy. Models of the demand for energy are presented in Section 6.4 and these models are estimated and the results analysed in Section 6.5. The conclusions to be drawn from this chapter are considered in Section 6.6.

6.2 *Trends in Energy Imports*

While imports of energy have provided the major source of energy used in the Irish economy over the period 1960 to 1982, any attempt to explain their trend over the period should take account of changes in domestic energy production.[10] In addition, for technical reasons, due to economies of scale in production or transportation, Ireland has re-exported a variable proportion of the energy imported into the country over the period. Table 6.1 gives details of the volume of energy accounted for by each of these categories. In the case of each kind of domestic energy production, because they were largely destined for use in generating electricity, they were converted into the amount of fuel oil[11] required to generate the same quantity of electricity. The resulting quantity of fuel oil was valued at its 1975 unit value (world prices plus the cost of transport to Ireland) to give a series at constant 1975 prices. This conversion into fuel oil was undertaken because, for most of the period, fuel oil was the marginal fuel used in generating electricity. The value of exports of energy[12] was deflated by the same import unit value as that used to deflate energy imports. As can be seen from Table 6.1, until the advent of domestic supplies of natural gas from the Kinsale field in the early 1980s, domestic production of energy was fairly stable. Exports of energy,

10. From 1979 onwards natural gas from a new domestic discovery became available to the Irish economy.
11. The data are given in FitzGerald (1987). The conversion factors are generally from Convery, Scott and McCarthy (1983). In the case of hydroelectric power one MWH (megawatt hours) is taken to be equal to 0.2765TOE at 31.1 per cent efficiency. Domestic supply is first converted into tonnes of oil equivalent (TOE) and aggregated. This aggregate is then converted to tonnes of fuel oil using the relevant conversion factor and the result is multiplied by the 1975 unit value for imports of fuel oil.
12. Export of energy excludes exports SITC 32 which consists largely of peat moss which is used for non-energy purposes. This item is also excluded from domestic energy production.

Table 6.1: *Production and Trade in Energy*

			Volume, £ Million, 1975 Prices:		
	Imports	Domestic Production	Energy Use – Gross	Exports	Energy Use – Net
1960	123.7	44.0	167.7	20.1	147.6
1961	130.1	45.6	175.7	16.2	159.5
1962	128.2	47.4	175.6	12.7	162.9
1963	131.1	45.4	176.5	15.2	161.3
1964	135.7	46.8	182.5	10.1	172.4
1965	147.7	40.2	187.8	13.5	174.3
1966	155.5	44.2	199.7	6.6	193.1
1967	185.8	46.3	232.1	29.4	202.7
1968	182.4	54.0	236.4	13.4	223.1
1969	198.2	50.2	248.3	15.0	233.3
1970	231.9	48.2	280.2	20.4	259.8
1971	262.7	44.7	307.4	17.9	289.5
1972	242.4	44.3	286.7	12.2	274.4
1973	270.7	38.1	308.8	12.0	296.8
1974	254.7	42.5	297.2	12.2	285.0
1975	243.7	57.1	300.8	13.7	287.1
1976	237.8	49.1	286.9	5.0	281.9
1977	260.2	47.2	307.4	6.2	301.2
1978	265.5	43.0	308.5	2.9	305.6
1979	297.4	45.1	342.5	4.1	338.4
1980	291.1	56.5	347.6	7.0	340.6
1981	260.7	73.4	334.0	5.9	328.1
1982	247.9	90.6	338.5	6.2	332.3

Sources: CSO *Trade Statistics of Ireland*, see FitzGerald (1987) for sources of domestic production.

on the other hand, fell from a peak in the mid-1960s. The development of transhipment facilities at Whiddy Island in the early 1970s did little to change this trend.

Energy imports and net domestic energy demand are expressed as a percentage of final demand in Table 6.2. While the ratio of imports of energy to final demand fluctuated between 4 and 5 per cent in the 1960s and early 1970s, showing no strong trend, the period after the first oil crises of 1973/74 saw a fairly continuous fall in the ratio. Its value of 3.1 per cent in 1982 is by far the lowest observation for the whole time period examined. The pattern displayed by the series for net domestic consumption of primary energy as a percentage of final demand shows a rather similar trend to that of the imports series except that the decline in the ratio after 1973/74 is less pronounced. The substantial fall in the imports ratio in 1981 and 1982 disappears in the net consumption series which takes account of the increased domestic energy production of those years.

Table 6.2: *Energy Usage, Volume*

	As a Percentage of Final Demand:	
	Total Imports	*Net Domestic Consumption*
1960	4.6	5.5
1961	4.5	5.5
1962	4.3	5.4
1963	4.1	5.0
1964	4.0	5.0
1965	4.2	4.9
1966	4.3	5.3
1967	4.9	5.4
1968	4.4	5.3
1969	4.4	5.2
1970	5.0	5.6
1971	5.4	6.0
1972	4.7	5.3
1973	4.8	5.2
1974	4.4	4.9
1975	4.3	5.1
1976	4.0	4.7
1977	4.0	4.6
1978	3.7	4.2
1979	3.8	4.4
1980	3.8	4.4
1981	3.3	4.1
1982	3.1	4.2

Source: Department of Finance Databank.

When the ratio of imports to weighted final demand was examined, the ratio was found to display an identical pattern of behaviour to the series in Column 1 of Table 6.2. This indicates that the fall in the energy intensity of final demand was not due to any change in the composition of final demand away from products with a high energy content. Instead, the explanation is to be found in changes in the production process itself, designed to economise on energy usage.

The share by volume of each source of primary energy in total gross[13] domestic energy consumption is shown in Table 6.3. The components of imports, coal, oil and gas, are all deflated by the unit value index for total

13. Imports plus domestic production.

energy imports. This use of a common deflator for all imports clearly biases the results. In the 1960s oil prices fell relative to coal prices. However, the absence of separate unit value indices leaves little alternative to this procedure but the potential effects on the results must be borne in mind in interpreting the data. This bias should not affect the overall breakdown between domestic production and imports.

Table 6.3: *Sources of Primary Energy as a Percentage of Total (Gross) Primary Energy Usage, Volume*

	Imported:			Domestic:				
	Total	Coal	Oil	Gas	Total	Coal	Peat	Gas	Hydro
1960	73.73	23.39	49.92	0.43	26.26	2.54	18.71	0.0	5.02
1961	74.04	24.28	49.55	0.21	25.96	2.42	19.61	0.0	3.93
1962	73.03	21.84	50.84	0.35	26.97	2.43	21.06	0.0	3.48
1963	74.29	22.58	51.27	0.44	25.72	2.47	19.88	0.0	3.36
1964	74.36	21.05	52.79	0.52	25.64	2.65	19.66	0.0	3.32
1965	78.62	20.91	57.24	0.47	21.38	1.97	15.45	0.0	3.96
1966	77.88	20.74	56.31	0.83	22.13	1.90	16.20	0.0	4.03
1967	80.05	17.09	62.50	0.46	19.94	1.70	15.19	0.0	3.06
1968	77.17	15.74	60.68	0.74	22.83	1.54	18.51	0.0	2.78
1969	79.80	15.17	63.69	0.93	20.20	1.27	16.90	0.0	2.03
1970	82.78	15.09	66.81	0.87	17.22	1.18	13.56	0.0	2.48
1971	85.45	11.82	72.68	0.95	14.55	0.62	12.62	0.0	1.31
1972	84.42	12.49	70.65	1.29	15.45	0.55	12.84	0.0	2.06
1973	87.65	10.55	75.72	1.38	12.35	0.44	10.10	0.0	1.81
1974	85.69	6.28	78.55	0.85	14.31	0.46	11.57	0.0	2.28
1975	81.01	5.06	74.69	1.26	18.99	0.34	17.16	0.0	1.50
1976	82.88	4.04	76.94	1.91	17.12	0.43	14.90	0.0	1.79
1977	84.66	5.89	76.69	2.08	15.34	0.37	12.86	0.0	2.11
1978	86.06	6.73	77.26	2.07	13.93	0.22	11.74	0.0	1.97
1979	86.82	7.02	77.94	1.86	13.18	0.39	8.73	2.0	2.06
1980	83.75	6.17	75.28	2.29	16.25	0.40	9.85	3.94	2.07
1981	78.03	6.98	68.84	2.21	21.97	0.44	11.45	7.87	2.21
1982	73.22	6.38	64.63	2.22	26.78	0.39	11.74	12.63	2.02

Source: See FitzGerald (1987).

As can be seen from Table 6.3, imports of oil, which only provided 50 per cent of domestic energy needs in the 1960s, rose to a peak in 1974 when they accounted for nearly 80 per cent. This growth in share occurred partly at the expense of imported coal and partly at the expense of domestic production, which remained static in absolute terms until the early 1980s. The growth in domestic production in the early 1980s, as the natural gas find came into production, significantly altered this picture, bringing dependence on external energy sources back to the level of the early 1960s. For the future, the new coal-fired electricity generating station, which has recently begun producing electricity, may result in some change in this picture. However, this is likely to be relatively small compared with the other changes which have taken place in the recent past.

6.3 The Role of Energy Imports in the Economy

Table 6.4 gives a breakdown of imported energy by the sector of the economy which first uses the imports (the sectors into which these imports occur as a primary input). The data are based on the 1975 input-output table. In the case of energy imports, over 80 per cent were used as an input into the productive sector of the economy in 1975. However, most of this underwent further transformation in either the oil refining or utilities sectors before being used to provide final energy, either to the rest of the productive sector or direct to consumers. When allowance is made for that portion of energy imports which passed directly to consumption from these two energy transformation sectors, the proportion of energy imports used as an input in the rest of the domestic production sector falls to around 60 per cent.[14] Thus, the demand for energy imports will be heavily affected by changes in the technology of the energy transformation sector and by factors affecting the demand for inputs in the rest of the productive sector. Therefore, the most appropriate aggregate model to describe energy demand in Ireland is one based on production theory rather than consumer theory. The factors affect-

Table 6.4: *Breakdown of Direct Demand for Energy Imports, 1975, per cent*

Agriculture:	Total	3.7
Industry:	Mining and quarrying	3.2
	Oil refining	39.3
	Manufacturing — other	9.8
	Utilities	12.6
	Building	4.3
	Total	69.2
Services:	Total	7.6
Productive sector:	Total indirect	80.5
Final demand:	Total direct	19.5

Source: CSO Input-Output Table as transformed by Murphy (1984).

14. Thirty-five per cent of the output of the oil refining sector passed directly to final demand as did 43 per cent of the output of the utilities sector.

ing the demand for energy will be changes in technology, changes in the prices of the different inputs, and the overall level of activity. Changes in the price of energy imports compared to the price of other consumer goods will play a less direct role in affecting energy demand. While a more disaggregated model could be developed which would take all of these factors into account, such a task is outside the scope of this paper.

6.4 Models of Energy Demand

From the point of view of consumers of energy the origins of the energy, whether domestic or imported, are irrelevant. The effect of a change in the domestic supply of energy is to change imports of energy directly. If the domestic supply of primary energy were constant this would not pose a serious problem. However, as indicated in Section 6.2, the increase in domestic supply due to the advent of natural gas had a significant effect on imports. To overcome this problem the total demand for primary energy, both domestic and imported, is modelled rather than energy imports *per se*. Energy imports are then derived from the following identity:

$$M3F = E - QE + XE \qquad (6.1)$$

where M3F = imports, SITC 3, at constant 1975 prices, £ million,
     QE = domestic production of energy, valued at constant 1975 prices, £ million,
     E   = total demand for primary energy, at constant 1975 prices, £ million,
     XE = exports of energy (SITC 33, 34 and 35), at constant 1975 prices, £ million.

Two approaches, described in Chapter 2, are tried to the problem of modelling total energy demand. The first approach uses the temporary equilibrium model, Equation 2.18 in Chapter 2. As indicated, the appropriate activity variable to use in that model is the volume of variable inputs (Brown and Christensen (1981)). In this chapter it is defined as the volume of (net) domestic consumption of primary energy at constant 1975 prices plus the volume of labour, valued at constant 1975 wage rates. The second approach adopted uses the vintage capital model described in Section 4 of Chapter 2. This model allows for the fact that the energy intensity of different vintages of the capital stock may differ and may not be altered after installation.

6.5 Results

These two models of energy demand were estimated and the demand for energy imports was in each case residually determined using the identity 6.1. The results of estimating the first or standard model are set out below.

As discussed in the previous section it assumes that energy, labour and capital can, to a limited extent, be substituted for one another after the capital stock has been installed and does not take account of the fact that substitution possibilities will be affected by the technical characteristics of the capital stock already in place.

$$E = -36.313 + QIV(.2248 + .1643(AAEI/PE)^{\frac{1}{2}} -$$
$$(0.7) \qquad (3.1) \qquad (6.2)$$

$$.003215(KIM(-1)/PE)^{\frac{1}{2}}) \tag{6.2}$$
$$(5.3)$$

$$\bar{R}^2 = .972 \quad S.E. = 11.1 \quad DW = 1.66 \quad DFFITS = 1.37$$

where E   = total domestic consumption of primary energy at constant 1975 prices, £ million. See Equation 6.1.

QIV   = variable inputs into industry at constant 1975 prices, £ million,

AAEI = average annual earnings in industry,

PE   = unit value index for imports SITC3,

KIM = capital stock in industry at constant 1975 prices, £ million.

Equation 6.2 provides a reasonably satisfactory fit. All the coefficients, barring the intercept, are significantly different from zero. The Durbin-Watson statistic is in the indeterminate region. The DFFITS statistic indicates that no one observation was unduly influential in determining the eventual result. Table 6.5 sets out the elasticities calculated on the basis of this equation. The own price elasticity is small, though correctly signed. The elasticity with respect to wage rates is positive, implying that labour and energy are substitutes. Its magnitude is rather large implying very substantial substitutability in the short term between labour and energy, a finding which conflicts with the results of many other studies such as that of Artus and Peyroux (1981). The elasticity with respect to the capital stock suggests that capital is energy saving. These results are, of course, conditional on the given level of the capital stock in each year. In the longer term, when the capital stock is allowed to vary in line with changes in factor prices, the elasticities could be considerably different from those shown here. Generally the results from this equation are rather implausible. The large elasticity with respect to wage rates is out of line with all other studies and counterintuitive. This probably reflects the rather unsatisfactory nature of the underlying model.

The vintage model of energy demand, discussed in Chapter 2, was also estimated and the results are described below. In this case it has been adjusted for autocorrelation by an appropriate transformation of the basic equation.

$$E = 0.933 \: [E(-1) - 0.516 \: E(-2)] + 0.322 \: [IN\{PK^*/PE^*\}^{0.661} -$$
$$ (30.4) (2.5) (4.8) (3.5)$$

$$0.516 \: IN(-1)\{PK^*(-1)/PE^*(-1)\}^{0.661}] + 0.516 \: E(-1) (6.3)$$
$$(2.5) (3.5) (2.5)$$

$$\overline{R}^2 = 0.999 \quad \text{S.E.} = 10.3 \quad \text{DFFITS} = 1.00$$

where PK* = expected cost of capital,
   PE* = expected cost of energy,
   IN = non-building investment, gross.

The equation was estimated by non-linear least squares using the TROLL Package. The fit is somewhat better than that for Equation 6.2. All the co-efficients are significantly different from zero at the 95 per cent level. Unfortunately, when the capacity utilisation variable[15] was included to reflect the

Table 6.5: *Elasticities Based on Equation 6.2*

	Elasticity of Energy Usage with Respect to:		
	Energy Prices	Wage Rates	Capital Stock
1960	−0.08	0.56	−0.48
1961	−0.09	0.56	−0.47
1962	−0.11	0.60	−0.49
1963	−0.12	0.64	−0.52
1964	−0.13	0.64	−0.51
1965	−0.13	0.66	−0.53
1966	−0.14	0.64	−0.50
1967	−0.15	0.65	−0.50
1968	−0.16	0.61	−0.45
1969	−0.18	0.63	−0.46
1970	−0.18	0.60	−0.42
1971	−0.18	0.55	−0.38
1972	−0.22	0.62	−0.40
1973	−0.23	0.62	−0.39
1974	−0.17	0.42	−0.25
1975	−0.20	0.43	−0.23
1976	−0.20	0.41	−0.20
1977	−0.20	0.40	−0.19
1978	−0.24	0.45	−0.21
1979	−0.22	0.39	−0.17
1980	−0.21	0.37	−0.15
1981	−0.21	0.35	−0.14
1982	−0.22	0.36	−0.14

15. This was defined as the ratio of actual output to trend output in manufacturing industry. Trend output was obtained by regressing output on a third order polynomial in time.

intensity of use of capital, it proved to be insignificant. As a result, it was dropped from the equation. This result carries the implication that either energy demand is invariant with respect to the utilisation of capital or that the variable used failed to measure it adequately. Factor specific technical progress was also ruled out when tested.

The depreciation rate estimated for the non-building capital stock was just under 7 per cent. This is a little lower than would be suggested by some evidence for other countries (Blades, 1983) but is none the less plausible. The elasticity of substitution between capital and energy is 0.66. These inputs are, by definition, substitutes. This elasticity is rather higher than the results obtained by Artus and Peyroux for a range of different countries using a rather similar model. However, their data sample ended in 1978 before the economies studied had time to fully adjust to the oil price shock of 1973. Results from two other cross country studies using a static model, though showing considerable variation across countries, produced results for the elasticity of substitution consistent with those found above (Griffin and Gregory, 1976 and Pindyck, 1979).

Decisions by investors on the energy capital ratio, which will be binding for the life of the asset, will be based on expectations of future prices rather than on actual current prices. In the case of this model, expected values have been proxied by the average of the current and two previous periods' observed prices. Attempts to replace these rather crude moving averages by modelling prices as a function of previous prices proved unsatisfactory. (The cost of capital series used incorporates a variable interest rate and ignores the effects of the tax shield due to depreciation allowances and tax relief on interests, see FitzGerald (1983).) Attempts to endogenise the scrapping rate along the lines of Artus (1983) also proved unsatisfactory.

The short-run elasticity of demand for energy with respect to its own price is shown in Table 6.6. (The elasticity with respect to the cost of capital is the same as that for energy prices with the sign changed.) It ranged from a peak of -0.11 in 1969 to a low of -0.03 in 1975. The short-run elasticity of energy imports with respect to its own price is also shown in Table 6.6. It is calculated on the assumption that domestic energy production and exports were unaffected by prices. Given the size of domestic energy production compared to exports, this elasticity is naturally somewhat higher than that of total energy demand. These results differ somewhat from those obtained from Equation 6.2, though the short-run elasticity in both cases is fairly low.

A true estimate of the long-run elasticity of energy demand with respect to its own price would require a complete model of the domestic productive sector. The possibility of substituting labour for the vintage capital energy bundle, in response to a rise in the price of the capital energy bundle, would

Table 6.6: *Elasticities Based on Equation 6.3*

	Elasticity of Energy Usage with Respect to Energy Prices:		Elasticity of Energy Imports with Respect to Energy Prices:	
	Short Run	Long Run	Short Run	Long Run
1960	−0.07	−0.61	−0.08	−0.73
1961	−0.08	−0.59	−0.10	−0.73
1962	−0.08	−0.58	−0.11	−0.74
1963	−0.09	−0.57	−0.11	−0.70
1964	−0.09	−0.57	−0.11	−0.72
1965	−0.10	−0.63	−0.12	−0.74
1966	−0.09	−0.58	−0.11	−0.72
1967	−0.08	−0.57	−0.09	−0.62
1968	−0.09	−0.53	−0.11	−0.65
1969	−0.11	−0.55	−0.13	−0.65
1970	−0.10	−0.52	−0.11	−0.58
1971	−0.08	−0.44	−0.09	−0.49
1972	−0.07	−0.41	−0.08	−0.46
1973	−0.08	−0.38	−0.09	−0.42
1974	−0.05	−0.29	−0.06	−0.33
1975	−0.03	−0.21	−0.04	−0.25
1976	−0.04	−0.24	−0.05	−0.29
1977	−0.05	−0.31	−0.06	−0.36
1978	−0.09	−0.48	−0.11	−0.55
1979	−0.10	−0.52	−0.11	−0.59
1980	−0.08	−0.48	−0.09	−0.56
1981	−0.07	−0.43	−0.08	−0.54
1982	−0.06	−0.43	−0.08	−0.57

have to be taken into account. In addition, the effects on the optimal or desired long-run level of output of any change in energy prices could not be ignored.

A crude estimate of the long-run own price elasticity of demand for energy can be obtained from Equation 6.3, if the two effects, described above, are ignored and if, in addition, the current capital stock is assumed to be equal to the desired capital stock, then the effect of ignoring the substitution effect and the output effect will bias downwards the resulting estimate of the long-run elasticity. The effect of the third assumption is not as clearcut. Overall the estimates obtained on this basis are likely to be on the low side.

On the above simplifying assumptions, elasticities, termed long-run elasticities, were calculated[16] and they are presented in Table 6.6. Because of the crude assumptions underlying them, they should be taken as only indications

16. These long-run elasticities are equal to the short-run elasticities divided by the ratio of non-building investment to the total non-building capital stock. In this case the non-building capital stock was assumed to be equal to the private non-building capital stock calculated using a 10 per cent depreciation rate (KNBPR10 in the Department of Finance databank).

of rough order of magnitude. The results indicate that the long-run price elasticity of total energy demand with respect to its own price fell from a high of - 0.63 in the mid-1960s to a low of - 0.21 in 1975 rising again to - 0.43 in 1982. This elasticity is somewhat lower than the value obtained by Scott (1980). However, as mentioned above, if incorporated into a more complete model of the economy the elasticity would be somewhat higher than shown here and possibly close to that of Scott. The speed of adjustment is determined by the depreciation rate, estimated in Equation 6.3, which implies that it will take ten years to replace half the existing capital stock. As the new energy-efficient capital stock is only introduced as the old plant is scrapped, this is the appropriate measure of the speed of adjustment. This rather slow speed of adjustment contrasts with that estimated by Scott (1980), where the mean lag was only one and a half years.

The results obtained from Equation 6.3 are much more plausible in terms of the slow speed of adjustment than those obtained from Equation 6.2 or Scott (1980). A cursory examination of the history of the Moneypoint electricity generating station project indicates that, at least in the field of electricity generation, the adjustment lags may be as long as ten to fifteen years. However, too much weight cannot be put on these long-term results, not only due to the restrictive assumptions made in obtaining them, but also because they are based on a data sample which only covers eight years immediately following the first oil crisis. It is only when data covering the whole cycle of adjustment to the first oil crisis become available, stretching into the next decade, that we will have a clear picture of the full long-run effects of the large changes in relative prices in the 1970s.

6.6 Conclusions

In modelling the determinants of energy imports one should model the demand for primary energy as a whole. This task is undertaken in a production theory framework appropriate to a variable, 80 per cent of which is used as an input in the domestic productive sector. The results of the vintage model, described in this chapter, indicate that the demand for energy imports was significantly affected by the price shocks of the 1970s. While the short-run elasticity of demand for energy is likely to be small, the long-run elasticity is likely to be quite significant. The speed of adjustment of energy demand towards its long-run optimal level is likely to be very slow. When this slow and complicated adjustment process is superimposed on the pattern of changes in the price of energy (relative to other goods) experienced over the last fifteen years it becomes clear that the task of forecasting future energy demand is a complex one. The analysis in this chapter indicates that the effects of the rise in energy prices in the 1970s are still being felt ten or fifteen years later. On this basis the recent sharp fall in the relative price of energy could be expected to have repercussions stretching well into the next decade. However, the fall in oil prices will only result in significant changes in the pattern of demand if the new low prices are expected to persist well into the future. At present it seems unlikely that this is the case and that firms will start installing new energy intensive equipment in the expectation of continued cheap energy far into the future. The situation was rather different after the two oil price shocks of the 1970s when the general expectation was that the era of cheap energy was over.

These results point to the importance for those involved in forecasting energy demand of taking account of the effects of changing relative prices and price expectations. The experience of other countries, reflected in a wide body of economic research, confirms this result. Consequently, the failure of the ESB to take this factor into account in preparing its own forecasts is a matter for serious concern.

Chapter 7

RESULTS – IMPORTS OF MANUFACTURED GOODS (SITC 5 TO 9)

7.1 Introduction

Of all the categories of imports considered in this study, imports of manufactured goods are far and away the most important; they account for between one half and two-thirds of all imports. Their behaviour in the past, and likely pattern of growth in the future, has important implications for all aspects of economic policy. The importance of the rapid growth in imports of manufactured goods over the last twenty years lies not just in its effects on the economy through the balance of payments constraint, but also through its effects on domestic output.

The most important question to be answered concerning manufactured imports is why they grew more rapidly than most other components of GNP over the period 1960 to 1982. In addition, the results of the analysis outlined in this chapter throw some light on the behaviour of the supply side of the Irish economy and have implications for the effectiveness of different aspects of economic policy.

Section 7.2 considers the trends apparent in the data for manufactured imports over the period. The growth of each of the different categories of manufactured imports is examined. In Section 7.3 the role of manufactured imports in the Irish economy is considered with a view to specifying an appropriate model of the determination of manufactured imports. Such a model is specified in Section 7.4 and the results of estimating this model are described in Section 7.5 and subjected to detailed analysis. Finally, the conclusions to be drawn from this analysis are summarised in Section 7.6.

7.2 Analysis of Past Trends

The most striking feature of any examination of trends in manufactured imports is their very rapid growth over the last twenty-five years. As can be seen from the data presented in Table 7.1 manufactured imports, which accounted for approximately 50 per cent of the volume of total imports in 1960, rose to two-thirds of the total in 1982. The average annual growth rate of the volume of manufactured imports over the period was 8.4 per cent compared to 6.9 per cent for the volume of total imports. This rate of growth

was also much greater than the rate of growth of final demand over the
period so that the ratio of imports to final demand rose rapidly. Over the
1960s the rise in the ratio was a full 9 percentage points of final demand. In
the 1970s the ratio showed a much less precipitous rise. It rose to a temporary
peak in 1973, a peak in the economic cycle. After a fall, as the economy
moved into recession in the mid-1970s, it reached a new peak in 1979. The
period since the last peak of economic activity in 1979 saw a further fall in
the ratio in 1980, a level which held for both 1981 and 1982. Clearly, there
is a strong cyclical pattern in the behaviour of the ratio of manufactured
imports to final demand with the cycle mirroring the cycle in overall economic
activity in Ireland.

Table 7.1: *Imports of Manufactured Goods, SITC 5 to 9, Volume*

| | Manufactured Imports as a Percentage of: | | |
	Total Imports	Final Demand	Scaled Weighted Final Demand
1960	50.1	12.7	12.7
1961	50.7	13.7	13.3
1962	52.9	14.5	14.0
1963	54.1	15.4	14.6
1964	57.6	17.7	16.4
1965	56.6	17.8	16.3
1966	56.7	18.1	16.8
1967	56.3	17.8	16.1
1968	58.7	19.5	16.8
1969	62.7	21.8	17.8
1970	61.8	21.2	17.3
1971	61.2	21.3	17.6
1972	62.2	21.3	17.1
1973	64.8	24.1	18.8
1974	64.4	23.0	18.2
1975	60.7	19.9	16.3
1976	63.5	22.6	17.6
1977	65.0	23.8	17.8
1978	67.0	25.7	19.1
1979	67.3	27.5	20.2
1980	66.4	25.9	19.4
1981	67.1	26.0	19.5
1982	67.1	25.2	19.3

Source: Department of Finance Databank.

This cyclical behaviour is superimposed on a fairly steady upward trend
in the penetration of the Irish economy by manufactured imports. While
there is a wide range of possible reasons for this development it is useful to

break them into two groups: the growth may be due to a shift in the pattern of final demand in favour of imported goods; alternatively it may be due to changes in the structure of the productive sector of the economy. To the extent that public tastes have shifted to goods which are either totally imported, or already have a higher import content, such as cars and consumer durables, the observed share of imports in final demand will increase. This change in the pattern of demand may be due to changing tastes, changing real incomes or, possibly, changing relative prices. The other group of possible explanations for the increased import penetration of the economy includes changes in the competitiveness of the Irish productive sector, technical progress or cyclical shortages or surpluses.

A crude methodology for distinguishing between these two sets of explanations, as outlined in Chapter 1, is based on the use of data drawn from the 1975 input-output table. If the structure of the economy were to remain unchanged over time, other than through changes in the pattern of final demand, the volume of imports could be derived for each year by weighting each component of final demand by its average import content, derived from the 1975 I-O table. In Table 7.1 the scaled ratio of actual manufactured imports to a suitably weighted final demand variable is shown. If there were no change in the structure of the economy due to competitiveness, technical progress, or cyclical factors, this ratio would be unchanged over time. To the extent that this ratio changes over time it is a measure of the increase in import penetration due to changes in the structure of the productive sector of the economy.

The difference between the change in the two ratios over any time period provides a crude measure of the rise in import penetration due to a shift in the pattern of final demand. As can be seen from Table 7.1 the (scaled) ratio of imports to weighted final demand rose by 6.7 points from 1960 to 1982 compared to a rise of 12.5 percentage points in the ratio of imports to unweighted final demand. This would suggest that a little under a half of the observed increase in import penetration was due to changes in the pattern of final demand with the residue being explained by changes, for whatever reason, in the structure of the domestic productive sector.

Even when the effects of changing demand patterns are allowed for in this way, the rise in import penetration due to changes in the productive sector of 6.7 points is still of considerable importance. The pattern of import growth over time attributable to the two different sets of factors is very similar, being much more rapid in the 1960s than in the 1970s or early 1980s.

Table 7.2 shows the distribution of manufactured imports by single digit SITC category, deflated by the overall deflator for manufactured imports, expressed as a percentage of weighted final demand (in volume). (The results

Table 7.2: *Manufactured Imports, Disaggregated, Scaled as a Percentage of Weighted Final Demand, Volume*

	Chemicals	Manufactures Classified by Material	Machinery and Transport Equipment	Miscellaneous Manufactures	Total Manufactures	Unclassified Including Shannon	Total
	SITC 5	SITC 6	SITC 7	SITC 8	SITC 5 to 8	SITC 9	SITC 5 to 9
1960	1.67	4.21	4.44	1.01	11.32	1.36	12.68
1961	1.64	4.32	4.86	1.08	11.89	1.57	13.46
1962	1.71	4.35	5.25	1.19	12.50	1.48	13.97
1963	1.83	4.44	5.44	1.29	13.00	1.61	14.60
1964	1.93	4.98	5.83	1.47	14.21	2.00	16.21
1965	2.03	4.59	5.83	1.44	13.88	2.13	16.01
1966	2.06	4.82	5.50	1.49	13.87	2.57	16.44
1967	2.04	4.59	5.27	1.55	13.45	2.41	15.86
1968	2.22	4.80	5.54	1.73	14.29	2.11	16.40
1969	2.06	4.94	6.65	1.81	15.47	1.80	17.27
1970	2.11	4.95	6.22	1.88	15.16	1.73	16.89
1971	2.22	5.00	6.43	2.06	15.71	1.60	17.31
1972	2.43	5.00	6.12	2.24	15.79	1.01	16.80
1973	2.71	5.57	6.76	2.32	17.37	0.94	18.31
1974	3.09	5.75	5.86	2.29	16.99	0.81	17.80
1975	2.67	4.63	5.83	2.19	15.31	0.72	16.04
1976	2.74	4.94	6.34	2.38	16.39	0.81	17.20
1977	2.78	4.79	6.71	2.39	16.66	0.78	17.44
1978	2.99	4.83	7.50	2.63	17.96	0.67	18.63
1979	3.18	5.24	7.81	2.91	19.14	0.57	19.71
1980	2.80	4.95	7.36	3.17	18.28	0.68	18.95
1981	2.89	4.71	7.54	3.21	18.34	0.66	19.00
1982	2.93	4.58	7.43	3.30	18.24	0.65	18.89

Sources: CSO *Trade Statistics of Ireland*; Department of Finance Databank.

have been scaled so that the ratios of total manufactured imports to weighted
and unweighted final demand in 1960 are identical.) The data in this latter
table give an indication of the change in the intensity of use of the different
categories of manufactured imports in the economy. As explained in Chapter 3
and FitzGerald (1987), the data are affected by a discontinuity in the available
trade series between 1971 and 1972. This particularly applied to the unclassified items in SITC 9.

As can be seen from Table 7.2 imports of chemicals grew strongly in the
mid-1970s. This occurred because of the growth of chemicals output consequent on the opening of a substantial number of new multinational enterprises. These firms used partially processed chemicals as inputs into their
production process. The impetus of this development fell off in the early
1980s with a consequential stabilisation in the ratio of this category of
imports to weighted final demand. Imports of goods SITC 6, which includes
textiles, paper and steel, rose in the late 1960s and early 1970s and have
tended to fall back between 1980 and 1982. As these imports are largely used
as an input into the manufacturing sector, these changes are indicative of
changes, for whatever reason, in the structure of that sector. Imports of
machinery and transport equipment, which are the largest single sub-category
of manufactured imports, rose fairly steadily over the 1960s and 1970s.
Miscellaneous manufactures have shown the most rapid rise of any category
of manufactured imports. As with machinery and transport equipment
imports, they rose steadily through the 1960s and 1970s. However, unlike the
other categories of manufactured imports, they continued to increase their
share of weighted final demand into the early 1980s. Finally, even allowing
for a discontinuity in the data, unclassified imports, including Shannon, have
tended to fall in significance since the mid-1960s. One of the major reasons
for their rise in the early 1960s was the growth of the industries on the
Shannon industrial estate, whose raw material imports are included in this
category of imports. In the 1970s the growth of Shannon was much less rapid
and this is reflected in the slowdown in unclassified imports. The other factor
affecting this category was the reclassification in 1972 whereby all temporary
imports were dropped from SITC Category 9 and included with permanent
imports in their relevant SITC class.

One further possible way of breaking down manufactured imports is to
extract imported capital goods from the total. The series for imported capital
goods is obtained from Table 10 in the National Accounts and deflated by
the deflator for total manufactured goods. As can be seen in Table 7.3,
expressed as a percentage of non-building investment, they increased their
share drastically over the period 1960 to 1982. However, the trend in the
ratio of capital goods imports to non-building investment differs greatly from

Table 7.3: *Imports of Investment Goods and Other Manufactured Goods*

	Imports of Investment Goods as a Percentage of:	Imports of Other Manufactures as a Percentage of:	
	Non-Building Investment	*Final Demand Excluding Inv. Non-Building*	*Weighted Final Demand Excluding Inv. Non-Building*
1960	62.6	10.6	65.5
1961	66.3	11.1	67.9
1962	67.5	11.7	71.8
1963	69.5	12.5	75.0
1964	69.8	14.8	87.1
1965	72.4	14.6	85.1
1966	74.4	15.0	88.1
1967	76.2	14.6	83.2
1968	76.0	16.0	87.5
1969	80.0	17.2	91.7
1970	77.7	16.8	89.4
1971	79.6	16.7	90.2
1972	71.5	17.3	90.6
1973	76.3	19.2	99.8
1974	68.7	19.2	99.2
1975	66.8	16.1	86.6
1976	71.1	18.1	93.7
1977	80.9	18.7	91.3
1978	80.4	20.4	100.0
1979	87.0	21.6	105.1
1980	89.3	20.4	99.4
1981	85.7	20.8	101.6
1982	84.6	20.3	100.7

Source: Department of Finance Databank.

the evidence in Table 1.3 in Chapter 1, drawn from successive input-output tables, which indicates that the total import content of non-building investment ranged between 71 and 74 per cent over the period 1964 to 1975. This contrasting behaviour suggests that the capital goods series may well include goods destined for other components of final demand. Certainly any attempt to use this classification to estimate a disaggregated model of the demand for manufactured goods proved unsatisfactory (see Section 7.4 of this chapter).

7.3 *Role of Manufactured Imports in the Economy*

In considering the role of manufactured imports in the economy two issues arise. First, where in the economy are the imports initially used? Second, in what products or components of final demand are these imports eventually embodied?

The data in Table 7.4, which are based on the 1975 input-output table, show that the proportion of total manufactured imports which were used as an input into the productive sector of the economy was 62.5 per cent. Only a little over one-third entered final demand without further transformation. As a result, this category of imports is probably best modelled as one of a number of factors of production used in producing a composite output, final demand.

Table 7.4: *Proportion of Manufactured Imports Used as Inputs in Each Sector in 1975, per cent*

Agriculture	2.2
Industry — manufacturing	49.1
— other	5.4
Services	5.8
Total indirect	62.5
Directly into final demand	37.5

While the manufacturing sector is by far the largest direct user of all manufactured imports, it still only accounted for half of the total used in the Irish economy in 1975. As a result, it is debatable whether this category of imports should be modelled as an input into the manufacturing sector alone or into the productive sector of the economy, treated as an aggregate. In the end, the decision between modelling manufactured imports as an input into the manufacturing sector or the aggregate productive sector was made on an empirical basis.

As well as considering the sectors into which manufactured imports first enter as an input, it is also important to consider what outputs, or components of final demand, account for the bulk of these inputs. Unless input-output separability is a valid assumption, changes in the composition of final demand can affect the demand for imports. As indicated in the previous section, such compositional changes appear to have been very important in the past in determining the propensity to import. As a result, it is important to identify those components of final demand which, due to their high manufactured import content, account for a high proportion of such imports. Table 7.5 shows what proportion of total manufactured imports ended up, directly or indirectly, in each component of final demand. This table is derived from the data in Table 1.3 by weighting the import content of each component by the proportion of final demand accounted for by that component in 1975. The resulting figures are then scaled to sum to 100 per cent. As can be seen from the table, non-building investment accounted for the largest proportion of manufactured imports, just under one-quarter; this sector was closely followed by industrial exports which accounted for 22.3 per cent of total manufactured imports. No other one component of final demand accounted for more than 10 per cent of the total. On the basis of these data, it may be useful when testing for input-output separability in modelling manufactured imports to subject non-building investment and industrial exports to special treatment.

Table 7.5: *Breakdown by Sector of Final Destination of Imported Manufactured Inputs, in 1975, as a Percentage of Total Manufactured Imports*

	%
Personal Consumption (including export tourism):	
Food	4.81
Alcoholic drink	0.99
Tobacco	0.53
Clothing and footwear	8.56
Fuel	0.56
Petrol	0.07
Durable household goods	5.50
Transport equipment	3.22
Expenditure abroad	0.00
Other goods	9.25
Other services	2.77
Public Consumption:	4.12
Investment:	
Building	7.20
Non-building	23.14
Change in Stocks:	
Agricultural	−0.34
Non-agricultural	0.68
Intervention	0.23
Exports:	
Agricultural	4.41
Industrial	22.30
Services (excluding tourism)	2.00

7.4 *The Model*

The "basic" temporary equilibrium model, outlined in Chapter 2, proved to be the most satisfactory in explaining the behaviour of manufactured imports. Attempts to use a vintage capital model, such as that used in Chapter 6 to model energy imports, resulted in an unsatisfactory statistical fit. The most general form of this equation tested is that shown below (7.1).

$$M59 = C1 + Q\,[C2 + C3(AAEI/PM59)^{\frac{1}{2}} + C4(PM3F/PM59)^{\frac{1}{2}} +$$

$$C5(KIM_{-1}/PM59)^{\frac{1}{2}} + C6/PM59^{\frac{1}{2}} + C7.CAPQ + C8.T] \qquad (7.1)$$

where M59 = manufactured imports (SITC 5-9) at constant 1975 prices, £ million,

Q = activity variable — this may be one of the following: the volume of output in manufacturing industry, final demand, weighted final demand or some component of final demand; all expressed at constant 1975 prices, £ million,

AAEI = average annual earnings in industry,

PM59 = index of price of manufactured imports,

PM3F = index of price of energy imports,

KIM = capital stock in manufacturing industry, constant 1975 prices, £ million,

CAPQ = index of capacity utilisation in manufacturing industry, 1975 = 1.0,

T = time,

C1 ... C8 = coefficients.

At its most basic this equation says that the propensity to import out of output is a function of a range of variables such as relative prices and capacity utilisation. If the coefficient C1 is equal to zero then this equation can be expressed in factor share form by dividing both sides by the activity variable Q. As discussed in Chapter 2, this is the standard form for the factor demand equations derived from a variable cost function, assuming that that function takes on the Generalised Leontief form. Homogeneity in factor inputs in the long run is imposed on the factor demand equation by imposing the restriction that coefficient C6 is zero. This restriction, together with the restriction on coefficient C1, were tested in the course of estimation and were not rejected by the data. (However, the imposition of homogeneity in the short term proves somewhat less satisfactory.) The inclusion of the time trend tests for the presence of factor specific technical progress. It could be replaced by some other variable, such as the rate of customs duties, which might affect, in a systematic way, the share of the different factors in total output. However, neither of these latter variables proved significant when tested in the equation. This equation differs from the standard factor demand equation, such as those estimated by Geary and McDonnell (1980) and Boyle and Sloane (1982) by the inclusion of the capacity utilisation term. The logic for including this term is discussed in Chapter 2. When output is above trend in this model, as measured by CAPQ, a higher proportion of final demand will be met from manufactured imports than would be the case if potential output had time to adjust fully. Conversely, low capacity utilisation may result in a fall in the share of imports in output or final demand.

The allowance made for the effects of disequilibrium in the level of output and the demand for capital does not preclude the possibility that the firms may have problems in adjusting imports to the desired level. However, tests with a simple dynamic structure, based on a partial adjustment model, suggested that this was not, in fact, the case.

The range of prices and, by implication, the range of factors of production included in Equation 7.1 was restricted to manufactured imports, energy, capital and labour. Initial attempts to include as separate factors, other import prices and the price of agricultural inputs into the industrial sector (proxied by agricultural output prices) did not prove satisfactory. Because of the problems in finding suitable proxies to measure them by, the effects of entrepreneurial input or management expertise could not be included as an explanatory variable. As a result, to the extent that they did affect the competitiveness of the Irish economy, they will not be taken into account in this specification. In interpreting the results from estimating the equation omitting such a factor, this must be taken into account.

When the actual levels of each price index for each year were replaced by a proxy for their expected levels, the fit of the resulting equation deteriorated. This result is consistent with a situation where firms are able to adjust their demand for manufactured imports very rapidly and can thus adjust quickly to price changes. They do not have to plan their purchase of imports years in advance, guessing at the likely prices of the different factors of production when the ordered imports are likely to arrive.

The choice of the appropriate activity variable is affected by two issues. First, are manufactured imports to be modelled as an input into the manufacturing sector or into the productive sector as a whole? Second, what assumptions are to be imposed concerning input-output separability; is the composition of output or final demand assumed to have an effect on the demand for imports? As outlined in the previous section, the evidence on the structure of the economy gives no clearcut answer on the first of these questions. However, in experimentation with the volume of output of manufacturing industry and the volume of final demand more satisfactory results were obtained with the latter variable.

A number of different approaches to the issue of input-output separability were tried. Two weighted final demand variables were used and the results compared to those obtained using unweighted final demand. The two sets of weights used were the manufactured import content of each component of final demand and the total manufactured goods content, both imported and domestically produced, of each component. The two weighted final demand variables produced markedly superior results to the unweighted variable. Of the two weighted variables, that using manufactured import weights proved the best. This result indicates that the assumption, implied by the use of unweighted final demand, that the propensities to import manufactured goods out of the different components of final demand are equal, is rejected in favour of the alternative pattern of (albeit rigid) unequal propensities, implied by the weighted variable. The full implications of the use of the weighted variable for the assumption of input-output separability were teased out in Chapter 2.

In addition to the relaxation of the input-output separability assumption implied by the use of the weighted final demand variable, experiments were made permitting the direct estimation of the propensity to import out of industrial exports and non-building investment. These two components of final demand were singled out for special treatment as they each accounted for between a fifth and a quarter of manufactured imports in 1975. The results from separating out non-building investment suggested that the assumptions implied by the use of the weighted final demand variable were, in fact, valid. In the case of industrial exports, its inclusion as a separate activity variable resulted in some improvement in fit and the estimated marginal propensity to import out of industrial exports was substantially greater, though not significantly so, than that implied by the alternative specification using the simple weighted final demand variable. It was this latter specification (7.2) which was finally chosen and is described below.[17]

$$M59 = FDWM59\ [C1 + C2(AAEI/PM59)^{\frac{1}{2}} + C3(PM3F/PM59)^{\frac{1}{2}} +$$

$$C4(KIM_{-1}/PM59)^{\frac{1}{2}} + C5.CAPQ] + C6.XI \qquad (7.2)$$

where FDWM59 = final demand, excluding industrial exports, with each component weighted by its manufactured imports content at constant 1975 prices, £ million,

XI   = industrial exports at constant 1975 prices, £ million.

The volume of imports required to produce a unit of industrial exports is equal to C6.XI and the demand for manufactured imports required to produce all other goods is equal to M59 – C6.XI. The equation can be transformed on this basis to a familiar factor share form where the dependent variable is (M59 – C6.XI)/FDWM59.

While the model described above assumes that manufactured imports as a group are separable from all other goods in the domestic production

---

17. An alternative version where the weight on industrial exports in the weighted demand variable was estimated, rather than imposed, produced marginally worse results than the specification adopted here, Equation 7.2.

process, some attempt was made to relax this assumption by estimating disaggregated equations for imports of capital goods, as defined in National
Income and Expenditure (Table 10), and all other manufactured imports.
This exercise was hampered by the fact that the only deflator available is
that for total manufactured imports. The results obtained were much less
satisfactory than those obtained from estimating the aggregate model. This
result cannot be construed as a test of the separability assumption, but it
does mean that one has little choice but to impose the assumption that manufactured imports are separable from all other inputs.

7.5 Results

The estimation of Equation 7.2 was carried out using instrumental variables[18] because of the endogeneity of some of the right hand side variables
in any underlying model of the economy. This naturally resulted in some
deterioration in fit but did not substantially alter the estimated coefficients.
Because of the inclusion of lagged variables as instruments, data were only
available for estimation for the period 1961-1982. The equation estimated
is shown below as 7.3.

$$M59 = FDWM59[-1.3684 + 0.3046(AAEI/PM59)^{\frac{1}{2}} +$$
$$\quad\quad\quad (5.1) \quad\quad\quad (3.1)$$

$$0.061(PM3F/PM59)^{\frac{1}{2}} + 0.0043(KIM_{-1}/PM59)^{\frac{1}{2}} +$$
$$(0.7) \quad\quad\quad\quad\quad\quad (1.4)$$

$$1.396\ CAPQ] + 0.4949\ XI \quad\quad\quad\quad\quad\quad\quad (7.3)$$
$$(6.9) \quad\quad\quad\quad (5.4)$$

$$\bar{R}^2 = .9998 \quad S.E. = 21.01 \quad DW = 1.55$$

The fit of this equation was extremely good, especially when compared
to the results for the other components of imports described in earlier chapters. While the Durbin-Watson is in the indeterminate region this is not
unusual given the number of parameters and limited number of observations.
When adjusted for autocorrelation the rho coefficient was not significant.

When estimated using OLS the DFFITS statistic was reasonably low indicating that no one observation had undue influence on the results. The strong
upward trend in the observed ratio of manufactured imports to final demand
(weighted or unweighted) which showed in the 1960s (see Section 7.2) might
suggest some change in behaviour over time, possibly due to freeing of trade.
However, as already mentioned, a customs rate variable proved insignificant.

18. The seven instrumental variables were: the prices of energy imports, manufactured imports, and
gross agricultural output, the volume of world exports of manufactured goods, the weighted final
demand variable and the capital stock, each lagged one period, and a constant.

The Chow tests for break in sample at either 1967, or 1973 (the year of EEC entry) did not suggest that any change in behaviour took place in those years. As reflected in this result, when the equation was estimated using data for the period 1967-1982 the coefficients, which were significant when estimated using the full sample, showed very little change in magnitude. As a result, it would appear that this equation and its coefficients are stable with respect to changes in data sample suggesting that its performance out of sample should also be satisfactory.

Four of the coefficients were highly significant. The two coefficients which were not significantly different from zero at the 95 per cent level, either separately or jointly, were those on the capital stock and energy prices. The coefficient on industrial wage rates was significantly positive indicating that labour and imports of manufactured goods are substitutes. In the case of energy prices the coefficient is also positive though insignificant. The coefficient on the capital stock, which is only significantly different from zero at the 20 per cent level, carries with it the implication that capital and imports of manufactured goods are, in the short run, complements. The coefficient on capacity utilisation in manufacturing industry was highly significant with the expected positive sign indicating that the propensity to import rises with the level of capacity utilisation.

Finally, the coefficient on industrial exports was highly significant. Attempts to parameterise the relationship between industrial exports and manufactured imports were unsatisfactory with all coefficients proving to be insignificant. As it stands the specification implies a constant propensity to import manufactured goods out of industrial exports ($\delta M59/\delta XI$) of 0.49. However, this value, while substantially higher than the input-output coefficient for 1975 of 0.35, is not significantly different from it at the 95 per cent level.

Table 7.6 shows the elasticity of manufactured imports with respect to their own price, the price of labour (AAEI), energy prices and the capital stock lagged one period. The own price elasticity is, as expected, negative falling from a high of - 0.34 in 1960 to a low of - 0.24 in 1982. The magnitude of the elasticity in 1982 is quite small, reflecting the fact that the short-run substitution effect of a rise in manufactured import prices is low.

The elasticity with respect to industrial wage rates, which is significantly different from zero, ranges between +0.22 and +0.18. This indicates that a deterioration in wage competitiveness leads to an increase in the use of imports and a higher import content in goods entering final demand. This substitution may take a wide range of forms. Within individual manufacturing enterprises there may be shifting of certain parts of the manufacturing process into or out of Ireland to minimise the worldwide cost of manufacturing. There may be straight substitution of more materials inputs for less labour, for example, due to the acceptance of higher wastage to minimise labour costs. At the distribution stage, retailers may substitute foreign produced goods for domestically produced goods (or vice versa) resulting in a change in the composite good (good including the distribution sector mark up) supplied to consumers.

Table 7.6: *Elasticity of Manufactured Imports with Respect to:*

	Own Price	Wage Rates	Capital Stock	Energy Prices
1960	−0.34	0.22	0.09	0.03
1961	−0.33	0.22	0.09	0.03
1962	−0.33	0.21	0.09	0.03
1963	−0.32	0.21	0.09	0.03
1964	−0.29	0.19	0.08	0.02
1965	−0.29	0.19	0.08	0.02
1966	−0.28	0.19	0.08	0.02
1967	−0.30	0.20	0.08	0.02
1968	−0.29	0.20	0.08	0.02
1969	−0.29	0.19	0.08	0.02
1970	−0.30	0.20	0.08	0.02
1971	−0.30	0.20	0.08	0.02
1972	−0.32	0.22	0.08	0.02
1973	−0.29	0.20	0.07	0.02
1974	−0.28	0.19	0.06	0.03
1975	−0.31	0.21	0.06	0.03
1976	−0.28	0.20	0.06	0.03
1977	−0.27	0.19	0.05	0.02
1978	−0.26	0.19	0.05	0.02
1979	−0.25	0.18	0.05	0.02
1980	−0.26	0.19	0.04	0.03
1981	−0.25	0.18	0.04	0.03
1982	−0.24	0.18	0.04	0.03

The elasticity with respect to energy prices is not significantly different from zero indicating that, at least in the short term, there is little possibility of substitution of imported manufactured goods for energy or vice versa. This result is consistent with the results for energy imports given in the last chapter.

The elasticity with respect to the capital stock is positive, though insignificant at the 95 per cent level. This suggests that, at least in the short term, changes in the capital intensity of the production process will have little effect on the demand for imports. As indicated earlier, in so far as it does affect the demand for imports the two factors are likely to be complements. These results indicate that it is only through its effects on the productive capacity and, hence, output that the capital stock influences the volume of imports.

It should be stressed that the above results must be construed as short-run elasticities conditional on a given capital stock and a given underlying productive capacity. To the extent that these are allowed to change, as they would in the longer term, the elasticity of demand for manufactured imports with respect to the other variables could vary.

Table 7.7: *Propensity to Import Manufactured Goods out of Weighted Final Demand*

	Total	Contribution of:			
		Wage Rates	Capital Stock	Energy Prices	Capacity Utilisation
1960	0.63	0.34	0.14	0.05	1.47
1961	0.70	0.35	0.14	0.05	1.53
1962	0.73	0.37	0.15	0.05	1.54
1963	0.74	0.38	0.15	0.05	1.53
1964	0.79	0.40	0.16	0.05	1.55
1965	0.76	0.40	0.16	0.04	1.53
1966	0.74	0.41	0.17	0.04	1.48
1967	0.77	0.43	0.17	0.04	1.50
1968	0.84	0.44	0.17	0.04	1.55
1969	0.88	0.46	0.18	0.04	1.57
1970	0.84	0.47	0.18	0.04	1.53
1971	0.84	0.48	0.18	0.04	1.50
1972	0.85	0.51	0.18	0.04	1.48
1973	0.95	0.52	0.18	0.04	1.57
1974	0.88	0.49	0.16	0.06	1.53
1975	0.78	0.49	0.15	0.06	1.40
1976	0.81	0.50	0.14	0.06	1.47
1977	0.85	0.50	0.14	0.06	1.51
1978	0.92	0.52	0.14	0.06	1.56
1979	0.99	0.54	0.14	0.07	1.62
1980	0.93	0.55	0.13	0.07	1.54
1981	0.92	0.56	0.13	0.08	1.52
1982	0.88	0.57	0.13	0.08	1.46

The marginal propensity to import out of weighted final demand implied by Equation 7.3 is shown in Column 1 of Table 7.7. In interpreting this statistic it should be remembered that if the marginal propensity to import out of each component of final demand were equal to the average propensity, derived from the 1975 input-output table (the weights used in the final demand variable), the marginal propensity to import out of weighted final demand would be equal to one for each year. In fact it was less than one in each year, growing rapidly in the 1960s from a low point of 0.63 to a high of 0.99 in 1979. Its upward trend in the 1970s was much slower than in the 1960s and it showed a much more erratic development over time. It is possible to decompose the changes in the total marginal propensity to import, shown in Column 1 of Table 7.7, into the contributions of the different exogenous variables included in the equation. This is done by evaluating separately each of the terms within square brackets in Equation 7.3 (e.g., the contribution of industrial wage rates is 0.3046 (AAEI/PM59)$^{\frac{1}{2}}$). When taken together with the intercept, – 1.3684, they sum to the marginal propensity to import shown in Column 1 of Table 7.7. This exercise shows that the driving force in the rise in the marginal propensity to import manufactured goods has been the deterioration in wage cost competitiveness. Changes in the capital stock and energy prices contributed little to the rise in the propensity to import over time. Changes in capacity utilisation from one year to the next clearly had substantial short-term effects on the propensity to import but, given the nature of the capacity utilisation variable, they could not have any long-term effect. It should be remembered that, as outlined in Section 7.2, a substantial part of the perceived rise in the propensity to import out of total (unweighted) final demand was due to changes in the composition of final demand. The analysis in that section suggested that approximately half of the rise in the ratio of manufactured imports to total final demand was due to compositional changes. The results given above suggest that the major explanatory variable for the rest of the trend rise was a disimprovement in the ratio of labour costs to import prices. Even if the absence of other variables, such as management expertise and entrepreneurial input, is allowed for, the change in labour cost competitiveness is still seen to have had a major role in the increase in the import penetration of the Irish market.

The results given above can be used to derive the marginal propensity to import out of the different components of final demand.[19]

The marginal propensity to import out of weighted final demand, obtained from solving Equation 7.3, is shown as the total propensity to import in Table 7.7. The marginal propensity to import manufactured goods out of industrial exports is, given the specification of Equation 7.3, fixed at 0.49.

---

19. The weighted final demand variable is a weighted sum of the components of final demand (F_i), excluding exports; it is defined in Equation 7.4.

$$FDWM59 = \sum_{i=1}^{n} w_i F_i \qquad (7.4)$$

where w_i are weights indexed over all components of final demand F_i. The marginal propensity to import out of any given component of final demand, holding capacity utilisation and the other right hand side variable unchanged, is then given by Equation 7.5. (CAPQ = $\overline{\text{CAPQ}}$ where CAPQ is treated as fixed at its historical value.)

$$\delta M59/\delta F_i \Big|_{\overline{CAPQ=CAPQ}} = (\delta M59/\delta FDWM59).(\delta FDWM59/\delta F_i)\Big|_{\overline{CAPQ=CAPQ}}$$

$$= \delta M59/\delta FDWM59 \Big|_{\overline{CAPQ=CAPQ}} . w_i \qquad (7.5)$$

However, this result is also conditional on capacity utilisation being treated as fixed in the short run. The marginal propensities to import out of each component of final demand, derived from Equation 7.5, are shown in the first three columns of Table 7.8.

Table 7.8: *Propensity to Import. Comparison of Results, With and Without Capacity Utilisation Fixed*

	Capacity Utilisation Fixed			Capacity Utilisation Variable		
	1975	1979	1982	1975	1979	1982
Personal Consumption (including export tourism):						
Food	0.07	0.09	0.08	0.49	0.61	0.49
Alcoholic drink	0.03	0.04	0.04	0.17	0.22	0.18
Tobacco	0.04	0.05	0.05	0.41	0.51	0.41
Clothing and footwear	0.37	0.51	0.45	0.57	0.75	0.64
Fuel	0.04	0.06	0.05	0.09	0.12	0.10
Petrol	0.01	0.01	0.01	0.08	0.11	0.08
Durable household goods	0.39	0.53	0.47	0.51	0.68	0.58
Transport equipment	0.32	0.44	0.38	0.49	0.64	0.55
Expenditure abroad	0.00	0.00	0.00	0.00	0.00	0.00
Other goods	0.43	0.58	0.51	0.58	0.77	0.66
Other services	0.05	0.07	0.06	0.08	0.10	0.09
Public Consumption:	0.05	0.07	0.06	0.08	0.11	0.09
Investment:						
Building	0.14	0.20	0.17	0.19	0.26	0.22
Non-building	0.50	0.68	0.60	0.62	0.83	0.72
Change in Stocks:						
Agricultural	0.06	0.09	0.08	0.16	0.21	0.17
Non-agricultural	0.39	0.53	0.47	0.61	0.80	0.68
Intervention	0.07	0.10	0.08	0.61	0.76	0.61
Exports:						
Agricultural	0.07	0.10	0.09	0.54	0.68	0.54
Industrial	0.49	0.49	0.49	0.93	1.03	0.92
Services (excluding tourism)	0.07	0.10	0.09	0.21	0.27	0.22

However, these propensities are heavily dependent on the assumption that capacity utilisation is fixed. If a change in weighted final demand is not matched by a similar change in the productive capacity of that industry, then capacity utilisation will rise. This will result in the measured marginal propensity to import being significantly greater than that shown in Table 7.7 or the first three columns of Table 7.8.

To calculate the marginal propensity to import, implied by Equation 7.3, on the assumption that the capacity of manufacturing industry is fixed in the short term requires an estimate of the effect on the actual volume of manufacturing output in the short term of an increase in each component of final demand (i.e., $\delta QGIM/\delta F_i$ where QGIM is the volume of output of manufacturing industry at constant 1975 prices). For illustrative purposes it may be useful to obtain values for $\delta QGIM/\delta F_i$ by assuming that they are equal to the average gross manufacturing output content of each component of final demand, derived from the 1975 input-output table. (For example, on average in 1975, a unit of industrial exports was associated with almost exactly one unit of gross manufacturing industry output.) This estimate is almost certainly an overestimate as it assumed that prices are held constant. To do otherwise would require a full model of the Irish economy, such as that of Bradley *et al.*, (1985). However, it allows one to determine the order of magnitude of the effects of assuming that capacity output is fixed. Using the input-output data discussed above to estimate $\delta QGIM/\delta F_i$ the value of the marginal propensity to import manufactured goods out of each component of final demand for the years 1975, 1979 and 1982 is shown in the last three columns of Table 7.8.[20] As can be seen from a comparison of the two sets of propensities to import in Table 7.8, the assumption concerning capacity utilisation has a crucial impact. In the case of industrial exports, if the increase in exports occurs because of a change in world demand without a corresponding increase in potential output the propensity to import will be extremely high, between 0.9 and 1.0. This is consistent with an underlying model of export determination where exports are largely supply determined rather than demand determined. The difference in the two sets of propensities to import for other components of final demand generally do not

---

20. Given the caveats specified in the text, the marginal propensity to import out of each component of final demand, holding capacity output constant, is derived in Equations 7.6 to 7.8.

$$\delta M59/\delta F_i = \delta M59/\delta FDWM59 \Big|_{CAPQ=\overline{CAPQ}} \cdot \delta FDWM59/\delta F_i$$
$$+ 1.396\,(\delta CAPQ/\delta F_i) \cdot FDWM59 \qquad (7.6)$$

When the capacity utilisation index is given by Equation 7.7,

$$CAPQ = QGIM/QGIMPOT.x \qquad (7.7)$$

where QGIMPOT = potential manufacturing industry output at constant 1975 prices, £ million. This is derived by regressing QGIM on a polynomial in time,
x = a constant for scaling,

then from Equations 7.6 and 7.7:

$$\delta M59/\delta F_i = \delta M59/\delta FDWM59 \Big|_{CAPQ=\overline{CAPQ}} \cdot \delta FDWM59/\delta F_i$$
$$+ 1.396\,\delta QGIM/\delta F_i \cdot (x.FDWM59)/QGIMPOT \qquad (7.8)$$

present as stark a picture as do those for industrial exports. However, they do make clear the fact that the effects on the volume of manufactured imports of a demand stimulus, which is not matched by an increase in potential output, is much greater than an increase in output stemming from an increase in productive potential. This has clear implications for demand management policy though a precise quantification of the effects would require a fully articulated model of domestic supply, something which is not attempted in this study.

7.6 *Conclusions*

The results described in this chapter clearly show that the trend rise in the ratio of manufactured imports to final demand over the period studied can be largely attributed to two factors: the changing composition of final demand and the rise in labour costs relative to import prices. The change in the composition of final demand, in particular the growth in importance of industrial exports, has led to a demand for manufactured goods of a kind not normally manufactured in Ireland. This growth has not taken place at the direct cost of any existing Irish producer. This trend, which is apparent in the Irish data, is commonly observed for other countries including the UK (Cuthbertson, 1985). From a policy point of view it means that there is little scope for cutting such imports other than through reducing the level of demand for the relevant categories of goods or through a major change in industrial policy.

In the case of the competitiveness variable, the measured short-run elasticity with respect to wage costs, while small, is none the less significant. It accounted for approximately half of the observed rise in the average propensity to import over the estimation period.

In considering the likely trend in the propensity to import in the future it is worthwhile considering the trends in the late 1970s and early 1980s. All the measures indicate that the effect of the changing composition of demand was much lower in that period than in the 1960s. It seems probable that this slowdown may continue as it is not possible for the components of final demand with a high import content to indefinitely increase their share of final demand. They must asymptote out at some point. The one variable to watch in this regard is industrial exports, which has a high growth rate and a high import content. In the case of competitiveness, future trends could clearly go in either direction depending on the stance and success of incomes policies.

The high propensity to import out of industrial exports is a matter for concern. When taken together with the substantial volume of profits which are repatriated, it suggests that domestic value added by new exporting industries is relatively small.

The significance of the capacity utilisation variable in determining the volume of imports is of importance not just in explaining short-term movements in the propensity to import. As spelt out in the previous section, it implies that the propensity to import out of a demand stimulus is much greater than out of a supply stimulus and that short-run demand management policy will have little effect on growth but a substantial effect on the volume of imports and the balance of payments.

Finally, the results indicate that imports are not readily substitutable for other factors of production, with the exception of labour. This result carries with it the implication that future growth in output will go hand in hand with increased imports of manufactured goods and that the scope for import substitution is strictly limited in the short run. However, in the longer term, the effect of changes in competitiveness on the level of potential output may enhance the effectiveness of measures designed to control domestic costs.

Chapter 8

RESULTS – IMPORTS OF SERVICES

8.1 *Introduction*

The single biggest problem in modelling services imports is the unsatisfactory nature of the data. It is impossible to obtain a continuous series for
the value of this category of trade and there are even greater problems in
determining the current price deflator to be used, both to determine the
volume of these imports and to explain their behaviour. However, the fact
that for most of the period examined, imports of services accounted for
between 7 and 9 per cent of all imports makes it impossible to ignore them.
In modelling these imports it was found desirable to disaggregate them into
other services imports and imports of tourism, where the latter covers expenditure outside the country by Irish residents on holiday abroad.

Section 8.2 of this chapter discusses the data and the trends which they show
over time. The role of this category of imports in the Irish economy is discussed
in Section 8.3 and the results of estimating the models for the two categories
of services imports are set out in Sections 8.4 and 8.5 and the conclusions to
be drawn from them are described in Section 8.6.

8.2 *Analysis of the Data*

Continuous series for Irish tourism imports (expenditure by Irish tourists
abroad) in value and volume terms can be derived from the Irish National
Accounts. However, the price deflator used to deflate the value of this expenditure is by international convention based on domestic consumer prices.
Clearly this convention is unrealistic in that this price is not the true price
paid by Irish holiday-makers. A more satisfactory, though complex, method
would be to deflate tourism imports by a weighted average of suitable price
deflators for the countries visited by Irish tourists.

The expenditure by Irish residents on transport to get to and from their
holiday destination, when made within Ireland, is not included in the item
for Irish tourist expenditure abroad. Instead, when payment is made within
Ireland to either a foreign or a domestic carrier it will, paradoxically, appear
as personal consumption expenditure on "travel within the State". Other
services imports then include all payments to foreign carriers, professional

and technical consultancy services, advertising abroad and other residual purchases of foreign services. This other services imports item is also deflated by Irish consumer prices to arrive at a volume series. However, even with the value series for other services there are a number of major problems: a number of components were treated on a net basis in the balance of payments statement prior to 1965. The revisions in the balance of payments statement in 1984, due to the use of exchange control and other records, was only properly carried back to 1975. Absence of information made only crude adjustments possible prior to that date. As a result, for years prior to 1975, the data on other services imports appear to be seriously deficient giving rise to an important discontinuity between the data up to 1974 and the data for 1975 to 1982.

As can be seen from Table 8.1 the share of services imports in total imports, which showed some stability in the 1960s, fell rapidly in the early 1970s up to 1974. In 1975 the share jumped by a substantial amount, probably due to improved data, as outlined above, rather than to any underlying change in circumstances. From 1975 to 1982 the share of services imports in total imports remained stable at its new higher level.

In examining the trend in the share of services imports in final demand account must be taken of the discontinuity between 1974 and 1975. This discontinuity could be due to either a steady deterioration in the coverage of services imports in the years up to 1974 which was arrested by the revision in the 1984 balance of payments statement or, alternatively, that as a result of new information, there was a once off improvement in coverage for 1975 and subsequent years. The latter appears to be the correct interpretation of the discontinuity and this was confirmed in the testing of different models in Section 8.5. On this basis, there appears to have been only a small increase in the share of services imports in final demand over the whole period. It rose to a peak in the mid-1960s falling back in the early 1970s and then rising to a new peak in 1979. The trend in the ratio of services imports to weighted final demand is rather different. It showed a clear increase within both sub-periods, 1960-1974 and 1975-1982. This indicates that when the changing pattern of final demand is taken into account there was some tendency for services imports to increase their market share. This increased import penetration was partially offset by the changing pattern of final demand where those categories of demand with a high services import content increased at a slower than average rate.

Table 8.2 shows the composition of services imports: tourism imports, payments for transport services and residual services imports, including payments for foreign professional and consultancy services. Separate data are only available for the last two categories since 1965. In the table the

THE DETERMINANTS OF IRISH IMPORTS

Table 8.1: *Imports of Services, Volume*

		Services Imports as a Percentage of:		
	Total Imports	*Final Demand*	*Weighted Final Demand*	*Scaled Weighted Final Demand*
1960	8.1	2.0	76.2	2.0
1961	7.9	2.1	79.1	2.1
1962	8.2	2.2	78.5	2.1
1963	8.3	2.4	79.7	2.1
1964	8.2	2.5	85.0	2.3
1965	8.5	2.7	89.2	2.4
1966	9.3	3.0	94.6	2.5
1967	8.4	2.6	92.9	2.5
1968	8.5	2.8	96.9	2.6
1969	7.5	2.6	97.1	2.6
1970	7.1	2.5	96.2	2.6
1971	6.7	2.3	96.8	2.6
1972	6.4	2.2	97.8	2.6
1973	6.1	2.3	98.3	2.6
1974	6.3	2.3	96.2	2.6
1975	9.6	3.1	125.6	3.4
1976	8.6	3.1	130.3	3.5
1977	9.0	3.3	139.1	3.7
1978	9.6	3.7	143.9	3.9
1979	9.1	3.7	133.2	3.6
1980	9.2	3.6	134.1	3.6
1981	8.6	3.3	135.1	3.6
1982	8.9	3.4	141.1	3.8

Source: Department of Finance Databank.

volume of each category of imports is expressed as a percentage of the volume of unweighted final demand. These data show that the problem, with a break in the series for services imports in 1975, is confined to the residual services category. Abstracting from the question of the break in the series, the data for tourism imports and residual services imports do not suggest any major increase in penetration by these two categories of imports of the Irish market over the 1960-1982 period. For imports of transport services there is some suggestion of an increase in the last five years of the period analysed, but even here the change is not clearcut or substantial. However, these data may also be affected by the use of inappropriate deflators. If the true deflator for tourism imports rose more slowly than the deflator used in the National Accounts (the Irish Consumer Price Index) then the volume of tourism services purchased would have grown more rapidly over the period. However, tests using, for example, the UK and Spanish consumer price indices, converted to Irish pound terms, did not substantially alter the picture.

Table 8.2: *Services Imports, Classified by Type, as a Percentage of Weighted Final Demand, Volume*

	Tourism and Travel (Excludes Passenger Fares)	Other Transportation	Residual Services
1965	64.09	18.30	6.84
1966	64.85	23.82	5.90
1967	63.13	23.66	6.07
1968	64.23	26.65	5.98
1969	62.47	28.23	6.40
1970	62.71	27.39	6.10
1971	62.47	28.39	5.95
1972	63.48	26.79	7.48
1973	64.84	26.57	6.87
1974	65.03	23.19	7.94
1975	66.90	23.30	35.44
1976	65.95	23.51	40.80
1977	65.38	28.85	44.88
1978	68.59	30.45	44.86
1979	71.33	27.74	34.14
1980	70.55	33.81	29.77
1981	69.40	34.88	30.87
1982	67.06	40.56	33.38

Source: Department of Finance Databank.

8.3 *Role of Services Imports in the Economy*

In considering the role of services imports in the Irish economy in the past twenty-five years it is useful to divide it into two roughly equal components, tourism imports and the residue, here termed "other services imports". These two different components have rather different determinants and are, as a result, probably best modelled separately.

Tourism imports are clearly a component of personal consumption and the factors governing its growth over time will be similar to those affecting the demand for all other categories of consumer expenditure. Over the full period, imports of tourism services in value terms increased their share of total consumption (in value) by a relatively small amount (see Table 8.3). The factors driving this albeit small and erratic increase were the change in the volume of total consumer expenditure and the prices of each component of consumer expenditure. Thus tourism imports should be modelled as part of a consumer demand system. The major problem facing such an approach is the difficulty in obtaining information on relevant price deflators. There are strong *a priori* grounds for believing that tourism imports are strongly complementary to the expenditure on access transport used to reach foreign

Table 8.3: *Share of Tourism Imports in Personal Consumption, Value*

	%
1960	3.10
1961	3.22
1962	3.51
1963	3.84
1964	3.99
1965	4.12
1966	4.38
1967	3.91
1968	4.13
1969	3.79
1970	3.62
1971	3.41
1972	3.24
1973	3.47
1974	3.57
1975	3.87
1976	3.68
1977	3.77
1978	4.35
1979	4.98
1980	4.73
1981	4.36
1982	4.30

Source: Department of Finance Databank.

holiday destinations. However, as mentioned above, this expenditure is included in the National Accounts in the wider aggregate "expenditure on travel within the State". Ideally what one would like is a price index covering the cost of the travel element of holiday expenditure but such data are not readily available for Ireland for the relevant period. The prices of other consumer goods and services which might potentially affect the demand for tourism imports should also be included in any model. However, in the absence of a suitable price index for the cost of home holidays, it is not clear what other commodities are likely to be close substitutes or complements to tourism imports.

In the case of other services imports the two components, imports of transport services and the rest of such imports covering professional services, etc., the driving forces may be rather different. The imports of professional services are largely used as an input into other sectors of the economy in the same way that imports of goods are used. In the case of the transport services imports, if they are used as an input into personal consumption of transport services, they will have a complementary relationship to tourism imports.

In so far as they appear as an input into the rest of the productive sector, they will be determined by the volume of external trade rather than by the overall level of activity. Thus in modelling other services imports as an aggregate they should probably be modelled as an input to the productive sector. However, as well as using the weighted final demand variable, used in earlier chapters, as the key activity variable, one might expect that a complementary relationship with the volume of trade would make the inclusion of a suitable trade variable desirable in any specification.

8.4 *Results – Tourism Imports*

In modelling the determinants of imports of tourism the AIDS model, described in Chapter 2, was used. The first problem to be faced in implementing this model was the choice of an appropriate price deflator for tourism imports. As the price deflator used in the Irish National Accounts is the Irish consumer price index it does not necessarily reflect the true price facing Irish holiday-makers. Not surprisingly, when tried in the model, it proved unsatisfactory. Studies carried out by Bord Failte (1984) indicate that in the 1970s and 1980s about one half of long holidays abroad were taken in the UK and the two other most important destinations were Spain and France. With this in mind experiments were carried out using combinations of Spanish and UK prices coverted to Irish pounds. Of the different variables tried, Spanish prices, when used as a proxy for Irish tourism imports' prices, gave the best fit. However, the implications of the estimated coefficients were not wholly satisfactory. An alternative version using UK prices, while giving a worse overall fit, had more plausible coefficients and is described below.

The choice of the other prices to include in the equation, and the separability assumptions which this choice implies, is restricted by the limited degrees of freedom available. The number of price variables in this case has been restricted to six: the own price, proxied by UK consumer prices in Irish pound terms, the price of alcohol, the price of motor vehicles, the price of entertainment, the price of travel within the State (excluding the cost of running motor vehicles but including the cost of foreign travel paid for within the State) and the price of the residue of consumption. Alternative breakdowns were tried including the prices of consumer durables, food, other services and other goods as separate arguments, but the results were unsatisfactory.

$$MTOVA/CV = -0.0665 - 0.0248 \log(PMTO/PCAR) - 0.0317 \log(PCAL/PCAR)$$
$$ (1.5) \quad (1.3) \quad\quad\quad\quad\quad (2.8)$$

$$+ 0.0937 \log(PCEN/PCAR) + 0.0216 \log(PCO/PCAR)$$
$$ (3.8) \quad\quad\quad\quad\quad (0.9)$$

$$- 0.024 \log(PCTR/PCAR) + 0.013 \log(CV/P) \qquad (8.1)$$
$$(2.4) \qquad\qquad\qquad (2.2)$$

$\bar{R}^2 = 0.761$ S.E. $= 0.00231$ DW $= 1.80$ DFFITS $= 2.29$

where MTOVA = the value of tourism imports, £ million,

CV = the value of total personal consumption, £ million. (This includes expenditure by foreign tourists in Ireland because of the problems in allocating this expenditure over the different components of consumption.)

PMTO = the price of tourism imports proxied by the UK CPI in Irish £ terms,

PCAL = the price of consumption of alcohol,

PCEN = the price of consumption of entertainment services,

PCO = the price of consumption of other goods and services,

PCTR = the price of consumption of travel services including travel within the State,

PCAR = the price of transport equipment (cars),

P = the price index for total consumption defined in Equation 2.34 in Chapter 2.

For an equation in share form the fit is not unreasonable. When the estimated share of imports of tourism services is converted into an estimate of the value and volume[21] of these imports the root mean square error is 6.77 and 4.73 respectively. These root means square errors compare favourably with the standard errors obtained for other categories of imports in earlier chapters. The Durbin Watson statistic, while in the indeterminate region, is quite high. The DFFITS statistic is very high indicating that one observation, that for 1979, is exerting significant leverage in the equation (Krasker, Kuh and Welsch, 1983). This is a cause for concern about the stability of the equation. When it was re-estimated for the 1965-1982 period there was little change in the results. However, when 1979 and subsequent years were dropped from the sample the results did show substantial change. As a result, the reliability of this equation out of sample must be seriously questioned.

The coefficients on the price of alcohol and the price of entertainment are both significant at the 5 per cent level. The coefficient on the price of residual consumption is not significant. The coefficient on the real total consumption variable, CV/P, is also significantly different from zero at the 95 per cent level.

The elasticity of tourism imports with respect to its own price (proxied by UK consumer prices), the prices of the other components of consumption

---

21. Using the deflator in the National Accounts.

and the volume of total consumption (the consumers' budget) are shown in Table 8.4. The derivation of the elasticities is shown in Appendix 3 together with the formulae for the standard errors of the elasticities. In the case of the own price, the elasticity is strongly negative for all years within the sample. While the coefficient on the own price in the estimated equation is not significant, this elasticity, which is affected by the coefficient on the budget variable, is significantly different from zero at the 95 per cent level for 1979 and 1980 and at the 90 per cent level for many of the other years including 1975.[22] The income elasticity or, more properly, the budget elasticity is greater than one which suggests that tourism imports are a luxury good – a plausible result. The coefficients on the prices of the other components of consumption indicate that tourism imports and consumption of cars, alcohol and travel are complements. When the income effect of changes in the prices of those goods is taken into account this effect is reinforced and the elasticities in Table 8.4 with respect to those prices are all negative. The elasticities with respect to the prices of entertainment and of other consumption are positive. In the case of consumption of entertainment services it is clearly a strong substitute for tourism imports. This is by no means surprising though the absolute size of the elasticity is rather too large to be plausible.

The results described above are based on the version of the model in which homogeneity was imposed. This assumption of homogeneity did not significantly alter the results. However, when symmetry was imposed and the whole system of demand equations were estimated together using FIML the fit of the equation for tourism imports deteriorated drastically.

When Spanish consumer prices were used as a proxy for Irish tourism import prices the results were somewhat different. The income or budget elasticity was less than one suggesting that tourism imports are a necessity rather than a luxury, a counterintuitive result. The own price elasticity was small, though negative, and not significantly different from zero. Consumption of entertainment appeared as a strong substitute for imports of tourism, just as it did in the equation described above. Generally, these results were implausible and, as Spain still accounts for only a minority of all tourist trips abroad, the equation using UK prices was preferred.

There are a number of potential sources for the problems encountered in modelling tourism imports: the inappropriate nature of the own price variables used in the National Accounts has already been highlighted. The alternative proxy variables tried here were themselves very unsatisfactory. Further research in this area might result in a significant improvement in results. While

22. The standard errors are calculated assuming homogeneity but ignoring symmetry and aggregation. See Appendix 3.

Table 8.4: *Elasticity of Tourism Imports with Respect to:*

	Own Price	Price of:					Budget
		Transport Equipment	Alcohol	Entertainment	Other Consumption	Travel	
1960	−1.88	−1.22	−1.14	3.26	0.38	−0.85	1.45
1961	−1.85	−1.18	−1.11	3.15	0.37	−0.83	1.44
1962	−1.78	−1.08	−1.01	2.88	0.34	−0.75	1.40
1963	−1.71	−0.99	−0.93	2.64	0.32	−0.69	1.37
1964	−1.69	−0.96	−0.90	2.56	0.31	−0.67	1.36
1965	−1.67	−0.94	−0.88	2.49	0.30	−0.65	1.35
1966	−1.63	−0.87	−0.82	2.33	0.28	−0.61	1.32
1967	−1.70	−0.98	−0.92	2.60	0.32	−0.68	1.36
1968	−1.66	−0.92	−0.87	2.46	0.30	−0.64	1.34
1969	−1.72	−1.00	−0.94	2.66	0.33	−0.70	1.37
1970	−1.74	−1.04	−0.98	2.76	0.34	−0.72	1.38
1971	−1.79	−1.10	−1.03	2.91	0.36	−0.76	1.41
1972	−1.82	−1.14	−1.07	3.03	0.37	−0.79	1.42
1973	−1.76	−1.07	−1.00	2.83	0.35	−0.74	1.39
1974	−1.74	−1.04	−0.98	2.75	0.34	−0.72	1.38
1975	−1.68	−0.95	−0.90	2.53	0.32	−0.66	1.35
1976	−1.72	−1.01	−0.95	2.66	0.34	−0.69	1.37
1977	−1.70	−0.99	−0.93	2.61	0.33	−0.68	1.36
1978	−1.61	−0.86	−0.80	2.26	0.29	−0.59	1.31
1979	−1.54	−0.75	−0.70	1.97	0.25	−0.52	1.27
1980	−1.56	−0.78	−0.73	2.07	0.26	−0.54	1.29
1981	−1.61	−0.85	−0.79	2.23	0.29	−0.59	1.31
1982	−1.61	−0.86	−0.81	2.27	0.29	−0.59	1.32

a range of price deflators for other components of consumption was tried, the absence of an appropriate price index for access transport was a serious deficiency. Finally, the assumption, not tested here, that imports of tourism can be treated as an aggregate may well be unwarranted. The item tourism imports includes both tourism to Britain, which probably has a strong habit element, due to the close ties between families in the two countries, and tourism elsewhere, which is likely to be much more responsive to changes in relative prices and the volume of consumption. When treated as an aggregate these two conflicting patterns of behaviour may seriously affect the results. It would seem desirable, if the data necessary to do so could be obtained, to model these two components separately and test the validity of the weak separability assumption maintained throughout the above analysis.

8.5 *Results — Imports of Other Services*

A number of experiments were tried assuming that this category of imports was complementary to merchandise exports, tourism exports, tourism imports or total foreign trade. This involved including these variables as separate independent arguments in the equation for other services imports. However, in each case these additional variables proved insignificant.

The activity variable used was a weighted final demand variable. As mentioned earlier, because of the difficulty obtaining a realistic own price deflator a fixed coefficient or Leontief type production function was assumed with no price variables as independent arguments. Because of the problem with the discontinuity in the data for other services imports, the propensity to import out of weighted final demand was allowed to alter at the breakpoint in the series. Finally, it should be remembered that the data prior to 1965 are generated data, as outlined in Chapter 3. As a result, care should be taken to ensure that the results obtained are not significantly affected by the inclusion of these early observations.

$$MOS = -53.0838 + FDWMOS(2.1042 + 0.9670D75) \qquad (8.2)$$
$$(7.6) \qquad\qquad (12.1) \qquad (15.1)$$

$$\overline{R}^2 = 0.991 \quad S.E. = 4.420 \quad DW = 1.51 \quad DFFITS = 1.92$$

where MOS   = volume of imports of other services at constant 1975 prices, £ million,

FDWMOS = weighted final demand variable where the weights are the other services import contents of each component of final demand, constant 1975 prices, £ million,

D75   = dummy, 0 up to 1974 and 1 thereafter.

This equation shows a reasonably good fit with all the coefficients being highly significant. While the Durbin Watson statistic is in the inconclusive region, when the equation was adjusted for autocorrelation, the rho coefficient was insignificant and the other coefficients were unchanged. Estimation dropping the first five years of the data sample, 1960-1964, produced very similar results to those shown above. The maximum DFFITS statistic value of 1.92 obtained for 1978 indicates that that observation might have exerted significant influence on the results giving rise to some doubts about the equation's stability out of sample. However, when the equation was estimated with data for the period 1960-1977 the results obtained were similar to those obtained using the full data sample.

The marginal propensity to import out of weighted final demand is 2.10 up to 1974 and rises to 3.07 thereafter. This rise is purely due to the discontinuity in the underlying data and does not reflect any change in the behaviour of other services imports. This propensity is very high. However, it must be remembered that the input-output weights used to generate the weighted final demand variable are based on the 1975 input-output table. This table is itself based on an earlier version of National Income and Expenditure (1977) which predates the upward revision in the other services imports series. While this estimated marginal propensity to import is significantly greater than the average propensity, it is constant over time. The addition of a time trend proved insignificant. As a result, the elasticity of imports of other services falls over time, as shown in Table 8.5, to a minimum of 1.37 in 1982. Clearly this elasticity will, on the basis of the above equation, fall further in future, tending to a long-run value of one.

Table 8.5: *Elasticity of Imports of Other Services with Respect to Weighted Final Demand*

	%
1960	5.40
1961	4.46
1962	4.85
1963	4.81
1964	3.60
1965	3.01
1966	2.49
1967	2.61
1968	2.31
1969	2.28
1970	2.34
1971	2.30
1972	2.24
1973	2.21
1974	2.36
1975	1.73
1976	1.63
1977	1.44
1978	1.28
1979	1.42
1980	1.42
1981	1.43
1982	1.37

8.6 *Conclusions*

The analysis of the determinants of imports of tourism services and other services is severely handicapped by data problems. The absence of plausible price deflators together with serious discontinuities in the data makes any modelling of these categories of imports very difficult. As a result, it is not surprising that the results obtained, in particular for tourism imports, are fairly unsatisfactory.

In the case of tourism imports, no matter what price variable was tried, domestic entertainment expenditure emerged as a significant competitor for allocation of consumers' expenditure. The results tend to confirm *a priori* expectations that price competitiveness does affect the volume of such expenditure. However, without further refinement it is difficult to quantify these effects with any certainty. While the income elasticity was significantly greater than one, this result was heavily dependent on the choice of UK consumer prices as a proxy for the price faced by Irish tourists abroad.

In the case of imports of other services, the marginal propensity to import out of weighted final demand is substantially greater than one though the effects of this on the volume of imports in the past has been partially offset by changes in the composition of demand. For the future, with a constant propensity to import, the elasticity of imports of other services with respect to weighted final demand will fall.

Chapter 9

RESULTS – TOTAL IMPORTS

9.1 *Introduction*

The determinants of each category of imports have been separately examined in Chapters 4 to 8. This chapter draws together these results to provide a comprehensive picture of the determinants of total imports. A single equation model of total imports is described in Section 9.2. This model is used to provide a yardstick against which the more sophisticated model, based on disaggregated equations, can be compared in Section 9.3. This comparison of the two models, single equation and multi-equation, covers both the overall fit and the general implications for the determinants of total imports. The results obtained from these models are themselves compared, in Section 9.4, with the results from earlier studies of the determinants of Irish imports. Finally, conclusions are set out in Section 9.5 concerning the appropriate model to use.

9.2 *Results for Total Imports – Single Equation*

Because of the fact that manufactured imports accounted for such a high proportion of total imports (between one half and two-thirds) the model chosen for total imports is the same as that used for manufactured imports:

$$MT = FDWMT \; [-0.631 + 0.306 \; (AAEI/PMT)^{\frac{1}{2}} + 0.0019(KIM(-1)/PMT)^{\frac{1}{2}}$$
$$\qquad\qquad (2.7) \quad (3.3) \qquad\qquad\qquad (0.7)$$

$$+ \; 0.133 \; (PM3F/PMT)^{\frac{1}{2}} + 0.833CAPQ] + 0.502XI \qquad\qquad (9.1)$$
$$\quad (1.4) \qquad\qquad\qquad (5.3) \qquad\qquad (3.7)$$

$$\bar{R}^2 = 0.9998 \quad S.E. = 27.56 \quad DW = 1.38$$

where AAEI   = average annual earnings in industry,

      CAPQ   = index of capacity utilisation in manufacturing industry, 1975 = 1.0,

      FDWMT = weighted final demand, excluding industrial exports, at constant 1975 prices, £ million. (The weights used are the total import content, direct and indirect, of each component of final demand derived from the 1975 I-O table.)

      KIM   = capital stock in manufacturing industry, constant 1975 prices, £ million,

MT   = total imports, at constant 1975 prices, £ million,
PMT   = index of price of total imports,
PM3F   = index of price of energy imports,
XI   = volume of industrial exports at constant 1975 prices, £ million.

Due to the endogeneity of some of the right hand side variables the equation was estimated using instrumental variables. With two exceptions the instruments used were the same as those used in estimating the equation for manufactured imports. (The exceptions were the replacement of the lagged weighted final demand variable appropriate to manufactured imports by the appropriate variable for total imports and the replacement of the price of manufactured imports by the price of total imports.) The fit of this equation is very good. While the Durbin Watson statistic is in the indeterminate region, when this equation was adjusted for first order autocorrelation, the rho coefficient was not significantly different from zero and the results were otherwise similar to those shown above. A Chow test for a break in the sample at 1967 or 1973 (because of the Anglo-Irish Free Trade Agreement or EEC entry) proved not to be significant. As in the case of the equation for manufactured imports, the coefficients on the wage rate, capacity utilisation and industrial exports were well defined. The imposition of homogeneity in the long run (see Chapter 2) and the dropping of an intercept from the equation was not rejected by the data. As a result, the equation can readily be expressed in factor share form.

In common with the specifications chosen for each of the components of imports, this specification resulted in a substantial improvement in fit compared to the results obtained from imposing strict input-output separability (i.e., using unweighted final demand or output). This result indicates that roughly 3.5 percentage points of the overall rise of 12.3 percentage points in the ratio of imports to final demand can be attributed to changes in the composition of demand. The residue, 8.7 percentage points, remains to be explained by the arguments appearing in Equation 9.1.

Table 9.1 shows the propensity to import out of weighted final demand implied by Equation 9.1 distinguishing the contributions to changes in the propensity over time from the different exogenous variables. As can be seen from this table, the propensity rose rapidly in the 1960s, largely because of the rise in wage rates *vis-à-vis* import prices. The change since the early 1970s has been much slower and has been primarily due to the effects of rising energy prices rather than to a loss of competitiveness due to rising labour costs. The capacity utilisation variable has a major effect on short-term variations in the propensity to import. Between 1975 and 1979 it added 0.13 points to the propensity to import. However, by definition, on its own, it has no long-term effect on imports.

Table 9.1: *Propensity to Import out of Weighted Final Demand from Equation 9.1*

	Total	Contribution of:			
		Wage Rates	Capital Stock	Energy Prices	Capacity Utilisation
1960	0.77	0.42	0.06	0.13	0.85
1961	0.82	0.44	0.06	0.13	0.89
1962	0.85	0.45	0.06	0.13	0.89
1963	0.85	0.46	0.06	0.13	0.89
1964	0.89	0.48	0.06	0.13	0.90
1965	0.87	0.49	0.06	0.12	0.89
1966	0.87	0.51	0.07	0.12	0.86
1967	0.90	0.53	0.07	0.12	0.87
1968	0.94	0.54	0.07	0.12	0.90
1969	0.97	0.56	0.07	0.12	0.91
1970	0.97	0.58	0.07	0.12	0.89
1971	0.98	0.60	0.07	0.12	0.87
1972	1.00	0.64	0.07	0.12	0.86
1973	1.05	0.64	0.07	0.12	0.91
1974	1.01	0.57	0.06	0.17	0.89
1975	0.93	0.59	0.06	0.16	0.81
1976	0.99	0.60	0.05	0.17	0.85
1977	1.01	0.60	0.05	0.17	0.88
1978	1.06	0.63	0.05	0.16	0.91
1979	1.13	0.64	0.05	0.18	0.94
1980	1.10	0.65	0.05	0.20	0.90
1981	1.10	0.65	0.05	0.21	0.88
1982	1.09	0.67	0.05	0.21	0.85

The elasticity of demand for total imports with respect to its own price, the prices of energy and labour (wage rates) and the capital stock are all shown in Table 9.2. The results are very similar to those for manufactured imports in Chapter 7. The own price elasticity of demand is, as is expected, negative. It falls from -0.37 to -0.31 over the period. The elasticity with respect to wage rates, which is significantly different from zero, ranges around $+0.25$ for the whole period indicating that labour and imports are substitutes for one another. While this elasticity is significant, it is not very high. However, it is only a short-run elasticity as it takes no account of the effects on the capital stock or output of changes in import prices or wage rates and through these variables, on imports in the long run. The elasticities with respect to energy prices and the capital stock are not significantly different from zero. In the case of energy the positive sign suggests that energy and imported materials are substitutes in the domestic production process. However, given the small magnitude of this elasticity, its statistical insignificance, and its short-run nature, it cannot be relied upon. The positive coefficient on the capital stock indicates a complementary relationship between capital and imports. However, this elasticity is also not significant, and, as a result, no great weight can be put on it.

Table 9.2: *Elasticity of Total Imports Implied by Equation 9.1 with Respect to:*

	Own Price	Wage Rates	Capital Stock	Energy Prices
1960	−0.37	0.26	0.03	0.08
1961	−0.36	0.25	0.03	0.07
1962	−0.36	0.26	0.03	0.07
1963	−0.35	0.25	0.03	0.07
1964	−0.34	0.24	0.03	0.06
1965	−0.33	0.24	0.03	0.06
1966	−0.33	0.24	0.03	0.06
1967	−0.33	0.25	0.03	0.06
1968	−0.33	0.25	0.03	0.06
1969	−0.33	0.25	0.03	0.05
1970	−0.34	0.26	0.03	0.05
1971	−0.34	0.26	0.03	0.05
1972	−0.36	0.28	0.03	0.05
1973	−0.33	0.26	0.03	0.05
1974	−0.33	0.24	0.03	0.07
1975	−0.35	0.26	0.02	0.07
1976	−0.33	0.24	0.02	0.07
1977	−0.33	0.24	0.02	0.07
1978	−0.32	0.24	0.02	0.06
1979	−0.31	0.23	0.02	0.06
1980	−0.32	0.23	0.02	0.07
1981	−0.31	0.22	0.02	0.07
1982	−0.31	0.23	0.02	0.07

9.3 *Results for Total Imports*

Having discussed the results obtained from estimating a single equation model of total imports this section examines the overall implications of the equations for each component of imports, described in earlier chapters of this paper, for the behaviour of total imports. The single equation model provides a useful yardstick against which the more sophisticated multi-equation model can be tested. The equations used for each category of imports are shown in Table 9.3.

Table 9.3: *Equations in Disaggregated Model of Total Imports*

SITC 0 and 1 (food and agricultural products):

$$M01 = 283.5 + CFOOD(.17 + .01D) + QAG(-1.34 + .20(PQAGG/PM01)^{\frac{1}{2}} +$$
$$.02(PF/PM01)^{\frac{1}{2}} + .23(KAG/EAG)^{\frac{1}{2}}) \tag{4.6}$$

SITC 2 and 4 (raw materials):

$$M24 = 2.394 + FDWM24(1.163-0.000167KIM) + IRB(0.148-0.118D) \tag{5.1}$$

SITC 3 (energy):

$$E = 0.933\,E(-1) + 0.322IN(PK*/PE*)^{0.661} \tag{6.3}$$

SITC 5-9 (manufactured goods):

$$M59 = FDWM59(-1.3684 + 0.3046(AAEI/PM59)^{\frac{1}{2}} + 0.061(PM3F/PM59)^{\frac{1}{2}} +$$
$$0.0043(KIM_{-1}/PM59)^{\frac{1}{2}} + 1.396\,CAPQ) + 0.4949\,XI \tag{7.3}$$

Imports of tourism services:

$$MTOVA/CV = -0.0665 - 0.0248\log(PMTO/PCAR) - 0.0317\log(PCAL/PCAR) +$$
$$0.0937\log(PCEN/PCAR) + 0.0216\log(PCO/PCAR) -$$
$$0.024\log(PCTR/PCAR) + 0.013\log(CV/P) \tag{8.1}$$

Imports of other services:

$$MOS = -53.0838 + FDWMOS(2.1042 + 0.9670D75) \tag{8.2}$$

The first test carried out was a within sample simulation of the multi-equation model. The period used for the simulation was restricted to 1962 to 1982 because of limited data availability for the energy imports equation. Table 9.4 shows the root mean squared error and root mean squared percentage error for total imports for the multi-equation model. These results are obtained from a single period simulation[23] of that model and are compared to the simulation results of the single equation model for the same period. As can be seen from this table, the multi-equation model provides a marginally better tracking performance than does the single equation model. The difference is not very substantial and does not suggest that the separability assumption involved in treating imports as an aggregate input into the production sector is necessarily invalid. However, the multi-equation model clearly allows for the possibility of a richer understanding of the factors driving the development of total imports over time and this additional information is not bought at the cost of overall explanatory power.

In Table 9.5 the short-run marginal propensity to import out of the different components of final demand from the two models are compared. These pro-

23. The historical value for the lagged dependent variable is used in the energy demand equation. The historical values of all right hand side variables are also used.

Table 9.4: *Comparison of Simulation Results of Multi-equation and Single Equation Models*

Model	Single Equation	Multi-equation
Root mean square error	24.12	23.23
Root mean square percentage error	2.00	1.62

pensities are calculated holding the capacity utilisation index constant. The implication of this assumption is that these propensities are only appropriate to the extent that increased demand for domestically produced goods is met by an identical increase in domestic supply. Generally, the propensities to consume, derived from the two different models of total imports, are reasonably close. This is not very surprising given the dominance of manufactured imports in total imports and the similar specification used for the equation for manufactured imports and the single equation model of total imports. Among the exceptions to the pattern of similarity are the propensities to import out of consumption of food, fuel and power, and petrol. In the case of food this result arises from the greater detail of the analysis of imports of agricultural goods (SITC 0 and 1) embodied in the multi-equation model. In the case of consumption of petrol and fuel and power it is due to a mismatch between the specification of the energy demand equation and the specification of the equations for the other categories of imports. Ideally, that part of domestic energy usage consumed directly by the personal sector should be separated out and modelled as a component of consumption, just as tourism imports are modelled. The rest of domestic energy usage could then be modelled using the vintage capital model described in Chapter 6. However, as it stands, because the investment variable described in Chapter 6 excludes investment in consumer durables, even in a complete model of the Irish economy, the propensity to import out of these two components of consumption would be underestimated.

In considering these results, it should be stressed that they are only short run in nature. They assume that capacity utilisation, factor prices and the capital stock are all fixed. An example of the importance of these assumptions is the case of industrial exports. As mentioned in Chapter 7, according to the 1975 input-output table, an average unit of industrial exports embodied a unit of gross industrial output. If this relationship is assumed to hold at the margin, holding the capital stock, potential output and factor prices constant, a unit increase in industrial exports in 1975 would have had the following effects on total imports depending on the model used:

single equation model 0.96;   multi-equation model   0.93

(This exercise involves endogenising the capacity utilisation variable in the manner described.)

This highlights the fact that industrial exports are essentially supply driven in the Irish economy and have generally been treated as such in macro-economic models (see Bradley *et al.*, 1981 and Bradley *et al.*, 1985). If supply does not rise to match an increase in demand the net effect of a change in industrial exports on the balance of payments will be totally offset by imports. While this result hinges on the crude assumption of a one to one relationship between industrial exports and industrial output this assumption is by no means implausible. A fuller examination of this issue would neces-sitate the simulation of these import models within the context of a full macro model of the Irish economy. The obverse of this analysis of industrial exports is the effect of an increase in potential or capacity output of manu-facturing industry in 1975 on total imports. *Ceteris paribus*, using the multi-equation model, this would have reduced total imports by 0.44 units. The question of what factors drive potential output and thus imports in the

Table 9.5: *Short-Run Marginal Propensity to Import out of Components of Final Demand (capacity utilisation held constant)*

Component		Single Equation Model	Multi-equation Model
Consumption	— Food	0.33	0.46
	— Alcohol	0.11	0.10
	— Tobacco	0.15	0.11
	— Clothing	0.53	0.49
	— Fuel and power	0.40	0.10
	— Petrol	0.36	0.06
	— Transport equipment	0.41	0.38
	— Durables	0.51	0.47
	— Other goods	0.58	0.53
	— Other services	0.09	0.15
Public Consumption		0.10	0.07
Investment	— Residential building	0.24	0.18
	— Other building	0.24	0.17
	— Non-building	0.64	0.55
Stock Changes	— Agricultural	0.23	0.07
	— Non-agricultural	0.66	0.44
	— Intervention	0.16	0.08
Exports	— Agricultural	0.17	0.09
	— Industrial	0.50	0.53
	— Services	0.29	0.38

longer term, is obviously also a case for treatment in the context of a fully articulated macromodel.

The last aspect of domestic supply influences on total imports to be considered is the effect of changes in net agricultural output. According to the multi-equation model, in 1962 the effect of a unit increase in the volume of net agricultural output on the volume of total imports would have been −0.5. By 1982 this had fallen to −0.2. This fall to a low level in 1982 is quite plausible given the change in orientation of Irish agriculture over the period, in particular since EEC entry. Today the bulk of increased agricultural output is destined for markets outside Ireland.

The elasticities of total imports with respect to the price of imports, wage rates and energy prices, calculated from both models, are shown in Table 9.6. (In the case of the own price elasticity for the multi-equation model the prices of all six categories of imports were simultaneously raised by 1 per cent.)

Table 9.6: *Elasticity of Total Imports with Respect to Factor Prices in 1975*

| | Model: | |
Price	Single Equation	Multi-equation
Price of imports	−0.30	−0.29
Wage rates	+0.21	+0.13
Price of energy imports, short run	+0.06	+0.01
Price of energy imports, long run	n.a.	−0.03

In examining these elasticities it should be remembered that they are drawn from an essentially short-run model of the demand for imports. Just as the propensities to import, discussed above, are conditional on a given level of output, a given capital stock and fixed factor prices, these elasticities are based on the same short-run model. With the exception of the equation for the demand for energy imports, they do not attempt to model the wider interactions relevant to an assessment of the impact of factor price changes on imports in the longer term.

In the case of the own price of imports there is little difference between the results from the two models. The elasticity is quite small though plausible in magnitude. It would be surprising if the economy could change its demand for imports rapidly as a result of major changes in the terms of trade. The elasticity with respect to wage rates in the multi-equation model is only just over half the value of the elasticity calculated from the single equation model. It is extremely low indicating that the instantaneous adjustment to a loss of competitiveness is small. However, in the equations in the multi-equation model in which wage rates appear they are significant so that the small size of the elasticity does not mean that it is not significant. To estimate the long-run elasticity would require information on the responsiveness of potential output and the capital stock to wage rates, something which is outside the scope of this paper.

The short-run elasticity of total imports with respect to energy prices is positive. This is due to the fact that demand for energy imports is slow to respond to changes in prices. As a result, while the own price elasticity of energy prices is, as theory would indicate, negative, it is dominated by the (insignificant) positive elasticity of manufactured imports. However, in the longer term the own price elasticity of energy imports with respect to its own price is much more strongly negative resulting in a small negative elasticity for total imports, as shown in Table 9.6.

9.4 *Comparison of Results with Results of Other Studies*

In this section the results, presented above, are compared to the results obtained by some of the previous studies of the Irish economy. In making such a comparison allowance must be made for differences in the dates with respect to which the elasticities are calculated, differences in data sample, differences in coverage, and differences in specification. The results for the other studies concerning the elasticity with respect to domestic activity, discussed in this section, must be considered short term in the same sense as the results set out in this paper; they assume an unchanged economic structure, in particular exogenous prices and an exogenous determination of capacity utilisation. The comparison of the results concentrates on those studies which presented information on their implications for total imports.[24] Because of the use of different classification systems for the disaggregation of imports, comparison of results at the more disaggregated level is difficult. Finally, the comparison of results in this section concentrates on the effects of changes in the activity variable and the own price term which, though differently defined, appear in all the studies examined.

A comparison of the elasticities of total imports with respect to the relevant activity variable in the different studies is set out in Table 9.5.[25] The results for the elasticity with respect to the activity variable differ considerably depending on the time period used in estimation and the precise specification chosen. The earlier studies which, perforce, used earlier data samples, had very much higher elasticities. The use of a weighted final demand variable served to reduce the estimated elasticity. However, the biggest dif-

24. Two recent studies, Lynch (1984) and O'Reilly (1985) presented no data on elasticities.

25. While the elasticities derived using different activity variables are not directly comparable one would expect that these differences should not greatly alter the results.

ference seems to lie between those studies which included a capacity utilisation variable and those which did not. In the cases where it is not included there is a degree of consistency between the results. Boylan *et al.* (1979), McAleese (1970) and Leser (1967) all suggest that the elasticity with respect to the activity variable is high. (In the case of this study, when Equation 9.1 was re-estimated without the capacity utilisation term this elasticity was substantially higher than when it was included.)

In the case of the studies which incorporated a capacity utilisation variable, the elasticities are less than 1. This is due to the fact that, given the specification, a substantial part of the effect of an increase in demand for imports comes through a rise in capacity utilisation. Thus, these results must be supplemented with estimates of the effects on imports through changes in capacity utilisation consequent on an increase in output, i.e., $\dfrac{\delta MT}{\delta CAPQ} \cdot \dfrac{\delta CAPQ}{\delta FDWMT}$.

The importance of this channel whereby domestic economic activity affects imports has generally not been adverted to by those studies for Ireland or elsewhere which used capacity utilisation as an explanatory variable. The fact that it is endogenous has not been taken into account in estimation or in quoting elasticities for imports with respect to the activity variable. Thus, the results shown in Table 9.7 for such studies must be taken as only a partial

Table 9.7: *Elasticity of Total Imports with Respect to Activity Variable*

Study	Activity Variable(s)	Year	Elasticity
This study Multi-equation model	Weighted final demand	1970	0.87
		1975	0.85
		1979	0.90
		1982	0.86
This study Single equation model		1970	1.01
		1975	1.00
		1979	1.04
		1982	1.05
FitzGerald 1979a*	Weighted final demand	1959	0.83 to 0.98*
		1976	0.85 to 1.01
Boylan *et al.*, 1979	GNP		1.56 to 1.79**
Kelleher & Sloane 1976	Weighted final demand		1.26
McAleese 1970	Output of TGI		2.10 to 2.15**
	Real disposable income		1.87 to 2.09
Leser 1967	GNP	1953-1963	1.61

*Range depending on low and high levels of capacity utilisation.
**Range depending on whether or not a lagged dependent variable is included.

view of the impact of changes in the propensity to consume and in the (implied) elasticity of imports with respect to the level of economic activity.

The results shown in Table 9.8 for the own price elasticity of imports show a less consistent pattern than do those in Table 9.7. The results from the earlier studies, and those using earlier data samples, tended to produce higher estimates of the own price elasticity than did the later studies based on data samples including the more recent period. With the exception of FitzGerald (1979a) and the production model of Geary and McDonnell (1980) the estimated own price elasticity was generally estimated at greater than −0.5. In a number of studies the own price term, and hence the price elasticity, was not significant (e.g., Lynch, 1984).

Table 9.8: *Elasticities of Total Imports with Respect to Own Price*

Study	Year	Equations	Elasticity
This study	1975	Multi-equation	−0.29
	1979		−0.23
	1982		−0.22
This study	1975	Single equation	−0.30
	1979		−0.27
	1982		−0.27
Geary and McDonnell 1980*	1954	Cost model	−0.48 to −0.62
	1960		−0.52 to −0.67
	1966		−0.55 to −0.71
	1972		−0.60 to −0.77
Geary and McDonnell 1980*	1954	Production model	−0.78 to −0.82
	1960		−0.66 to −0.68
	1966		−0.49 to −0.47
	1972		−0.33 to −0.32
FitzGerald 1979a	1976		−0.19
Boylan *et al.*, 1979			−0.56 to −0.68
Kelleher & Sloane 1976			−0.59
McAleese 1970		Real disposable income	−0.89 to −1.53
		Output of TGI	−0.91 to −1.25
Leser 1967			−1.38

*Elasticity of imports of materials for further production outside agriculture.

In the case of Kelleher and Sloane (1976) they had considerable difficulty finding a significant price term. The results from both the single equation and multi-equation models described in this paper show a much lower own price elasticity than most other previous studies, with the exception of FitzGerald (1979a). The similarity between the results in FitzGerald (1979a) and this study is not too surprising, given the rather similar approach adopted in the two studies. This elasticity must, as indicated earlier, be recognised as a short-term elasticity conditional on a fixed capital stock. If the capital stock is assumed variable, as in Geary and McDonnell, the substitution possibilities are greatly increased and the longer-run elasticity can potentially be much higher. This helps explain the higher elasticities obtained by Geary and McDonnell (1980) though not the higher elasticities obtained in other studies.

No comparable results are available from other studies for the effects of changes in wage rates, the capital stock, or energy prices on total imports. The Geary and McDonnell data on elasticities of substitution suggest that capital and imports are complements. The conclusion of this study is similar, though this result is not firmly based, given the insignificance of the estimated coefficient on the capital stock in Equation 9.1 and the equation for manufactured imports in Chapter 7. Both Geary and McDonnell and this study suggest that labour and imports are substitutes. However, the results in this paper are conditional on a given capital stock and could, theoretically, be altered when capital is allowed to vary in the longer term.

9.5 Conclusions

The above analysis indicates that the multi-equation model performed marginally better within sample than did the single equation model. With the exception of energy imports the multi-equation model is, like the single equation model, a short-term model. The results are conditional on the existing levels of the capital stock, output and prices. However, in spite of these similarities, the multi-equation model provides a richer explanation of the factors affecting the determination of imports.

The detailed conclusions concerning the determinants of Irish imports are set out in the final chapter of this paper.

Chapter 10

CONCLUSION

10.1 *Introduction*

Section 10.2 of this chapter summarises the results of the paper. It describes the reasons for adopting the precise model specification used in analysing each category of imports. The lessons learned from this analysis concerning the determinants of Irish imports are teased out. The final section of the chapter examines the policy implications of these results.

10.2 *Conclusions — the Determinants of Irish Imports*

The results at both an aggregated and a disaggregated level indicate that input-output separability must be rejected in modelling the demand for imports in Ireland: the composition of output or final demand has had a major influence on the behaviour of imports over the past twenty-five years. The pattern of development of the economy over the period, with the major growth in the importance of industrial output and exports, has resulted in a substantial increase in import penetration. This growth involved a major increase in the capital stock, much of which consisted of imported machinery and equipment. The new industry depended heavily on the use of imported raw materials. The fact that increasing wealth has led consumers to seek a wider choice of products and to devote an increasing share of their incomes to goods which are not produced in Ireland has also resulted in increased import penetration. All of these factors would have resulted in a substantial increase in import penetration even if there had been no change in the competitive position of the Irish economy over the period. The results in Chapter 9 suggested that almost a quarter of the rise in import penetration between 1960 and 1982 was attributable to this change in the composition of demand. The results in Chapter 7 suggested that approximately half of the rise in manufactured imports stemmed from this factor.

As indicated in Chapter 9, the question of whether imports as a group are separable from all other inputs is not decisively answered: the disaggregation of imports into six different categories, which were each determined by separate equations, did not produce markedly better results than the aggregate approach. However, the disaggregate model permits a much richer understanding of the factors driving imports in the past and the possibility of an improved understanding of how changes in the economy will affect the volume of imports in the future.

The results of this study indicate that the volume of imports is affected by changes in the price of imports relative to the price of other inputs, especially that of labour. This result rejects the hypothesis, maintained by some input-output models, that imported inputs are strongly separable from all other inputs (that the propensity to import is not affected by relative prices). While the plausibility of value added separability was not formally tested, the results suggest that it is not justified in the context of the Irish economy: changes in the capital labour ratio or in the relative prices of labour and other non-imported inputs can affect the volume of imports.

With the exception of the equation for energy imports, the model used to estimate the demand for the different categories of imports is essentially a short-run model. It cannot answer questions concerning the long-run impact of changes in relative factor prices. To do so, the results described in the paper need to be set within the context of a more complete macroeconomic model of the Irish economy. In saying this it does not mean that it needs to be incorporated into a fully specified framework, such as that described by Bradley *et al.*, (1985) although that would be very desirable. It is sufficient that one have an understanding, in qualitative terms, of how the economy as a whole behaves.

The results indicate that while agents in the economy choose their level of imports, conditional on the level of the existing capital stock, the level of imports is also affected by the extent to which the existing capital stock or output is different from the long-run optimal level of output. In estimation this shows up as a highly significant cyclical effect on the propensity to import. The results also indicate that, with the exception of energy imports, imports generally adjust very rapidly to what may be termed their temporary equilibrium level (conditional on the given capital stock).

While the short-term effects on imports of changes in competitiveness, in particular wage cost competitiveness, are relatively small (the elasticity with respect to wage rates is between 0.13 and 0.21), the cumulative effects are quite large. This study suggests that the deterioration in labour cost competitiveness had a major effect on the propensity to import throughout the period. This is especially the case for the 1960s, when the rapid rise in the propensity to import was primarily due to a relative rise in labour costs. In the case of manufactured imports the results of this study suggest that this loss of competitiveness probably accounted for nearly half of the observed rise in the propensity to import out of final demand over the twenty-three years 1960-82. Any long-run effects on the productive capacity of the disimprovement in competitiveness must be added to these short-run effects to arrive at the final effect on the economy. The evidence from Bradley and FitzGerald (1987) suggests that this cumulative long-run effect on the productive capacity can be quite large.

One obvious additional factor affecting the rise in the propensity to import over the sampe period was the freeing of trade. From the beginning of the period there was a progressive dismantling of barriers to trade with the outside world. The Anglo-Irish Free Trade Agreement (AIFTA) of 1965 provided for the progressive reduction of tariffs on imports of certain commodities from the UK from 1966 onwards. The entry of Ireland into the EEC in 1973 resulted in a further substantial reduction in tariff barriers between 1973 and 1977. McAleese and Martin (1973) suggested that the AIFTA added at least 1 per cent to the volume of imports by 1970. In this paper it did not prove possible to estimate a significant effect on imports from this source. For EEC entry this study suggests a substantial effect on the volume of food imports. It is estimated that, by the end of the period, food imports were a minimum of a quarter higher than they would have been under the trading regime in force prior to 1973. In the case of manufactured imports no significant impact from EEC entry was found. This is not to say that there was none, but rather that it was not sufficiently large to be detected, given the problems of modelling its impact. Taken together these results suggest that, with the exception of food imports, the AIFTA and EEC entry did not on their own have a major impact on the propensity to import.

This paper, in reinterpreting the significance of the capacity utilisation variable, makes clear the importance of domestic supply factors in determining the level of imports. If domestic supply is increased by some policy measure, holding demand constant, capacity utilisation falls resulting in a fall in imports. The policy implications of this result are dealt with in the next section.

The results of this paper suggest that the propensity to import out of industrial exports is quite high.

Conclusions concerning individual components of imports are as follows:

Imports of Food (SITC 0 + 1): Food imports rose considerably due to EEC entry. This does not necessarily mean that the economy suffered as a result of this increase: account must be taken of the wider choice made available to consumers through the reduction of import controls and also of the effects of farmers switching production to areas where profitability was enhanced through EEC entry. Whatever its effects on national welfare, the effects of EEC entry on the propensity to import were completed by the early 1980s and the propensity to import food should stabilise in the latter half of the decade. Changes in the composition of final demand tended to reduce the propensity to import food but this effect was more than offset by the changes consequent on EEC entry. The result of an increase in domestic agricultural output on food imports is, as expected, negative. However, this effect, which was quite large in 1960, had fallen to a low level by 1982 as the Irish agricultural sector shifted most of its capacity to producing for export rather than the home market.

Imports of Raw Materials (SITC 2 + 4): The results for this category of imports were unsatisfactory. They indicated that the propensity to import fell over time due to changes in industrial structure. However, this result was not firmly based and changes in industrial structure in the future could reverse this trend. However, this category of imports accounted for only 3.5 per cent of total imports in 1982.

Imports of Energy (SITC 3): The volume of energy imports is affected by changes in relative prices. In 1982 the long-run own price elasticity was estimated to be around - 0.6. The economy takes a long time to adjust to changes in real energy prices. The failure to take account of this slow speed of adjustment may have accounted for the failure to detect significant price elasticities in many earlier studies.

Imports of Manufactured Goods (SITC 5-9): Just over half the rise in the propensity to import manufactured goods out of final demand over the twenty-three years 1960-1982 was due to changes in the composition of final demand. A deterioration in labour cost competitiveness, especially in the 1960s, was the other major factor in the rise in the propensity over time. The propensity to import manufactured imports out of industrial exports was very high at around a half. The own price elasticity of manufactured imports was estimated to be - 0.24 in 1982. The elasticity with respect to wage rates was +0.18 at the same date. The results indicated that changes in domestic supply could have a substantial negative effect on the propensity to import.

Imports of Services: The results for the imports of services were not very satisfactory. In the case of tourism (expenditure by Irish tourists abroad) the estimates suggested an income elasticity greater than 1 together with some sensitivity to the domestic price of entertainment. However, because of data problems no great faith can be put in these particular results.

10.3 *Conclusions — Policy Implications*

(i) The first major policy question which arises from these results is what is likely to happen to the propensity to import in the future? Henceforth the change in the composition of final demand, which was so important in the rise in the propensity up to 1982, is likely to prove much less important. Industrial exports are unlikely to raise their share of final demand greatly. If they were to do so, it would imply a move to a surplus on the balance of payments which would, in any event, eliminate fears concerning the size of our import propensity. In the case of non-building investment, some rise in share might be possible. However, providing such investment is undertaken on sound financial criteria, its longer-term impact will be to increase supply and reduce imports. In the case of consumption, the tendency to reduce the share of expenditure on food and, therefore, the propensity to import food, is likely to continue. While a detailed medium-term forecast of future developments in the pattern of final demand would be necessary to produce firm forecasts of the movement of the propensity to import, the above discussion indicates that there will be little or no stimulus to the propensity to import from changes in the composition of final demand in the medium term.

Clearly, changes in the competitiveness of Irish industry could affect the propensity to import. They played a significant role in raising the propensity to import in the 1960s though their effects in the 1970s were somewhat smaller. In the absence of a compositional effect the development of competitiveness in the late 1980s will be the major potential source of any increase in the propensity to import, or conversely, of its reduction.

(ii) The second major policy implication to be drawn from this study is that a stimulus to output from fiscal policy will result in a substantial rise in the propensity to import above its pre-existing level. The multiplier effects of such stimuli will, as a result, be small as is evidenced by a number of other studies of the Irish economy (Bradley *et al.*, 1981; FitzGerald and Keegan, 1982; Bradley *et al.*, 1985). On the other hand, policies which result directly in an increase in the potential output of the Irish economy will have a much bigger effect, due to their lower impact on the volume of imports. Even as a short-term demand management measure, demand stimuli to the Irish economy, will have little effect on output and, by implication, employment serving only to raise capacity utilisation and, as a result, the volume of imports. For example, if capacity utilisation in 1982 had been raised to its 1979 level by a fiscal stimulus, imports would have been almost 10 per cent above their actual level.

(iii) The third major policy question which arises from this study is the question of what are the benefits to the Irish economy from the growth in industrial exports? The estimated propensity to import out of a unit change in industrial exports is very high. When taken together with the large repatriation of profits by foreign owned companies, this implies that the benefits to the Irish economy from such exports are not very great. As a result, the contribution to domestic value added from a unit of industrial exports is relatively small and it is a major cause for concern whether we are paying too much in terms of state subsidies and tax write offs for these exports.

(iv) The fourth major policy question which arises from this study concerns energy imports. The results indicate that in forecasting future energy demand it is important to take account of changes in relative prices. Large and costly mistakes will be made if this is not done in the future. The economy takes a long time to adjust to relative price changes and is still adjusting to changes in prices in the 1970s. As a result, current trends in energy demand are not necessarily a good indicator of trends in the medium to long term.

In conclusion, the results of this study suggest that the propensity to import, through its effects on the balance of payments, will not pose as big a constraint on the Irish economy in the medium term as it did in the past twenty-five years. Provided the ill-fated policies of demand stimulation, popular over the 1970s and early 1980s are avoided, we can look forward to more balanced growth in the future. The problem of raising the Irish growth rate can only be tackled by policies which raise the output potential of the Irish economy. This may seem platitudinous but, in the light of past history, clearly needs repetition.

REFERENCES

ARTUS, P., and C. PEYROUX, 1981. "Fonctions de Production avec Facteur Energie: Estimations pour les Grands Pays de l'OCDE", *Annales de l'Insee*, No. 14, Oct-Dec.

ARTUS, P., 1983. "Capital, Energy and Labour Substitution: the Supply Block in OECD Medium Term Models", OECD Working Paper No. 2, Paris.

BAKER, T.J., J. DURKAN, and J.P. NEARY, 1969 and 1970. "A Study of Imports", *Quarterly Economic Commentary*, May, September and December 1969, March and December 1970.

BELSLEY, D.A., E. KUH, and R.E. WELSCH, 1980. *Regression Diagnostics: Identifying Influential Data and Sources of Collinearity*, New York: John Wiley and Sons.

BERNDT, E., C. MORRISON, and C. WATKINS, 1981. "Dynamic Models of Energy Demand: An Assessment and Comparison", in E. Berndt, B. Field (eds.), *Modelling and Measuring Natural Resource Substitution*, Mass: Massachusetts Institute of Technology.

BLADES, D., 1983. "Service Lives of Fixed Assets", OECD Working Paper No. 4, Paris.

BORD FAILTE EIREANN, 1985. *Home Holidays 1984*, Dublin: BFE.

BOYLAN, T., M. CUDDY, and I. Ó MUIRCHEARTAIGH, 1979. "The Irish Aggregate Imports Demand Equation: the 'Optimal' Functional Form", *The Economic and Social Review*, Vol. 10, No. 2, pp. 147-156, January.

BOYLE, G.E., and P.D. SLOANE, 1982. "The Demand for Labour and Capital Inputs in Irish Manufacturing Industries, 1953-1973", *The Economic and Social Review*, Vol. 13, No. 3, pp. 153-170.

BRADLEY, J., C. DIGBY, J. FITZGERALD, O. KEEGAN, and K. KIRWAN, 1981. "Description, Simulation and Multipliers Analysis of the MODEL-80 Econometric Model of Ireland", Department of Finance Research Paper, 2/81.

BRADLEY, J., C. FANNING, C. PRENDERGAST, and M. WYNNE, 1985. *Medium-Term Analysis of Fiscal Policy in Ireland: A Macroeconometric Study of the Period 1967-1980*, Dublin: The Economic and Social Research Institute, General Research Series, No. 122.

BRADLEY, J., and J.D. FITZGERALD, 1987. "Industrial Output and Factor Input Determination in an Econometric Model of a Small Open Economy", *European Economic Review*, forthcoming.

BROWN, R.S., and L.R. CHRISTENSEN, 1981. "Estimating Elasticities of Substitution in a Model of Partial Static Equilibrium: An Application to US Agriculture, 1947 to 1974", in E. Berndt and B. Field (eds.), *Modelling and Measuring Natural Resource Substitution*, Mass: Massachusetts Institute of Technology.

BURGESS, D.F., 1974a. "A Cost Minimization Approach to Import Demand Equations", *Review of Economics and Statistics*, Vol. LVI, No. 2, pp. 225-234.

BURGESS, DAVID F., 1974b. "Production Theory and the Derived Demand for Imports", *Journal of International Economics*, Vol. 4, pp. 103-117.

CONVERY, F., S. SCOTT, and C. McCARTHY, 1983. *Irish Energy Policy*, Dublin: National Economic and Social Council Report No. 74.

COPELAND, J.R., and E.W. HENRY, 1975. *Irish Input-Output Income Multipliers 1964 and 1968*, Dublin: The Economic and Social Research Institute, General Research Series, No. 82.

CUTHBERTSON, K., 1985. "The Behaviour of UK Imports of Manufactured Goods", *National Institute Economic Review*, No. 113, August.

DEATON, A., and J. MUELLBAUER, 1980. "An Almost Ideal Demand System", *American Economic Review*, Vol. 70, No. 3.

DENNY, M., and M. FUSS, 1977. "The Use of Approximation Analysis to Test for Separability and the Existence of Consistent Aggregates", *American Economic Review*, Vol. 67, No. 3.

DEPARTMENT OF FINANCE, 1974. *Review of 1973 and Outlook for 1974*, Dublin.

DIEWERT, T.E., 1974. "Applications of Duality Theory", in M.D. Intrilligator and D.A. Kendrick (eds.), *Frontiers of Quantitative Economics*, Vol. 2, Amsterdam: North Holland.

DEPARTMENT OF ENERGY, 1984. *Report of the Inquiry into Electricity Prices*, Dublin.

FITZGERALD, J.D., 1978. "The Revised EEC Format Input-Output Table for Ireland 1969", Department of Finance Research Paper.

FITZGERALD, J.D., 1979a. "The Determinants of Irish Imports", Department of Finance Research Paper.

FITZGERALD, J.D., 1979b. "Estimation of a Consistent Set of Trade Figures on a BOP Basis", Department of Finance Research Paper.

FITZGERALD, J.D., 1983. "Comment on Paper on the Cost of Capital in Ireland by Flynn and Honohan", Department of Finance Research Paper.

FITZGERALD, J.D., 1984. "The Determination of Manufacturing Industries' Output in Open Economies", Department of Finance Research Paper.

FITZGERALD, J.D., 1987. *Consistent Trade Data for Ireland*, Dublin: The Economic and Social Research Institute, Technical Paper, No. 3.

FITZGERALD, J.D., and O.P. KEEGAN, 1982. "The Behavioural Characteristics of the MODEL-80 Model of the Irish Economy", *Journal of the Statistical and Social Inquiry Society of Ireland*, Vol. XXIV, Part IV, pp. 41-84.

FITZGERALD, J.D., O.P. KEEGAN, A. McQUAID, and A. MURPHY, 1983. "Department of Finance Databank of Economic Time Series", Department of Finance Research Paper, 2/83.

FITZGERALD, J.D., and A. McQUAID, 1983. "Generating the Databank", Department of Finance Research Paper, 3/83.

FITZGERALD, J.D., T. QUINN, B. WHELAN, and J. WILLIAMS, 1987. "The Effects of Differences in Rates of Indirect Taxation on Trade in Consumer Goods across the Republic of Ireland-Northern Ireland Border", Report for the European Commission, ESRI Mimeo.

FLYNN, J., and P. HONOHAN, 1984. "Notes on the Cost of Capital in Ireland", *IBAR*, Vol. 6, No. 1, April.

GEARY, P.T., and E.J. McDONNELL, 1980. "Implications of the Specification of Technologies: Further Evidence", *Journal of Econometrics*, Vol. 14, pp. 247-255.

GOLDSTEIN, M., and M.S. KHAN, 1985. "Income and Price Effects in Foreign Trade", in R.W. Jones and P.B. Kenen (eds.), *Handbook of International Economics*, Vol. II, Amsterdam: Elsevier Science Publishers.

GREEN, M.J., and P. LeGRANTEC, 1976. *Community Input-Output Tables 1970-75 Methodology*, Luxembourg: Statistical Office of the European Communities.

GRIFFIN, J., and P. GREGORY, 1976. "An Intercountry Translog Model of Energy Substitution Responses", *American Economic Review*, Vol. 66, pp. 845-857.

HALL, R.E., 1973. "The Specification of Technology with Several Kinds of Output", *Journal of Political Economy*, Vol. 8, No. 4, July/August, pp. 878-892.

HELLIWELL, J., and R. McCRAE, 1981. "Output, Potential Output and Factor Demands in an Aggregate Open Economy Model with Energy and Capital Bundled Together", working paper, University of British Columbia.

HENRY, E.W., 1972. *Irish Input-Output Structures 1964 and 1968*, Dublin: The Economic and Social Research Institute, General Research Series, No. 66.

HENRY, E.W., 1980. *Irish Input-Output Structures 1976*, Dublin: The Economic and Social Research Institute, General Research Series, No. 99.

IRELAND, *Industrial Production Index*, various issues, Dublin: Stationery Office.

IRELAND, *Statistical Abstract*, various issues, Dublin: Stationery Office.

IRELAND, *Trade Statistics*, various issues, Dublin: Stationery Office.

IRELAND, "Census of Agricultural Production", *Irish Statistical Bulletin*, various issues, Dublin: Stationery Office.

IRELAND, 1970. *Input-Output Tables for 1964*, Dublin: Stationery Office.

IRELAND, 1978. *Input-Output Tables for 1969*, Dublin: Stationery Office.

IRELAND, 1983. *Input-Output Tables for 1975*, Dublin: Stationery Office.

IRELAND, 1984. *National Income and Expenditure, 1982*, Dublin: Stationery Office.

IRELAND, 1984. *National Income and Expenditure, 1970-82*, Dublin: Stationery Office.

IRELAND, 1985. *Census of Industrial Production, 1980*, Dublin: Stationery Office.

JOHNSTON, J., 1972. *Econometric Methods*, Tokyo: McGraw Hill.

KEEGAN, O., 1984. "Description Simulation and Analysis of an Excise Tax Forecasting Model for Ireland", Dublin: The Economic and Social Research Institute, Mimeo.

KEEGAN, O., and A. MURPHY, 1983. "An Application of AIDS to Irish Consumption Data", Department of Finance Research Paper.

KELLEHER, ROBERT, and PETER SLOANE, 1976. "Import Demand Equations", Dublin: Central Bank of Ireland, Technical Paper 13/RT/76, December.

KHAN, MOSHIN S., and KNUD Z. ROSS, 1977. "The Functional Form of the Aggregate Import Demand Equation", *Journal of International Economics*, Vol. 7, No. 2, pp. 149-160.

KOHLI, U.R., 1978. "A Gross National Product Function and the Derived Demand for Imports and Supply of Exports", *Canadian Journal of Economics*, XI, No. 2.

KRASKER, W.S., E. KUH, and R.E. WELSCH, 1983. "Estimation for Dirty Data and Flawed Models", in Z. Grilliches and M.D. Intrilligator (eds.), *Handbook of Econometrics*, Vol. I, Amsterdam: North-Holland.

LEAMER, E.E., and R.M. STERN, 1970. *Quantitative International Economics*, Boston: Allyn and Bacon.

LESER, C.E.V., 1967. *A Study of Imports*, Dublin: The Economic and Social Research Institute, General Research Series, No. 38.

LYNCH, D., 1984. "Determining Irish Merchandise Imports", Dublin: Central Bank of Ireland, Technical Paper 1/RT/84, January.

McALEESE, DERMOT, 1970. *A Study of Demand Elasticities for Irish Imports*, Dublin: The Economic and Social Research Institute, General Research Series, No. 53.

McALEESE, D., and J. MARTIN, 1973. *Irish Manufacturing Imports from the UK in the Sixties: The Effects of AIFTA*, Dublin: The Economic and Social Research Institute, General Research Series, No. 70.

MacFADDEN, D., 1978. "Cost, Revenue and Profit Functions", *Production Economics. A Dual Approach to Theory and Applications*, Amsterdam: North-Holland.

MIT, 1983. *TROLL Reference Manual*, Third Edition, Boston: MIT.

MURPHY, A., 1984. "Analysis of the 1975 Input-Output Tables", Department of Finance Research Paper, March.

NADIRI, M.I., and S. ROSEN, 1969. "Interrelated Factor Demand Equations", *American Economic Review*, Vol. 59, pp. 456-471.

NORTON, D., 1984. "Smuggling under the CAP: Northern Ireland and the Republic of Ireland, 1974-82", Policy Paper No. 11, Department of Political Economy, University College, Dublin.

O'CONNOR, R., and E.W. HENRY, 1975. *Input-Output Analysis and its Applications*, London: Charles Griffin and Co. Ltd.

O'REILLY, L., 1985. "Determining Irish Merchandise Imports", Dublin: Central Bank of Ireland, Technical Paper, 4/RT/85, June.

PINDYCK, R., 1979. "Inter-fuel Substitution and the Industrial Demand for Energy", *Review of Economics and Statistics*, May, pp. 169-179.

REVENUE COMMISSIONERS, *Report of the Revenue Commissioners*, various issues.

SCOTT, S., 1980. *Energy Demand in Ireland, Projections and Policy Issues*, Dublin: The Economic and Social Research Institute, Policy Research Series, No. 2.

SUNDARARAJAN, V., and S. THAKUR, 1976. "Input-Output Approach to Import Demand Functions: Experiments with Korean Data", IMF Staff Papers, November, pp. 674-698.

THURSBY, J., and M. THURSBY, 1984. "How Reliable are Simple, Single Equation Specifications of Import Demand?", *Review of Economics and Statistics*, Vol. LXVI, No. 1, pp. 120-128.

UNITED NATIONS, *National Accounts*, various issues, New York.

VAN BOCHOVE, C.A., 1982. *Imports and Economic Growth*, The Hague: Martinus Nijhaff Publishers.

WINTERS, L.A., 1984. "Separability and the Specification of Foreign Trade Functions", *Journal of International Economics*, Vol. 17, pp. 239-263.

WINTERS, L.A., 1985. "Separability and the Modelling of International Economic Integration", *European Economic Review*, Vol. 27, pp. 335-353.

Appendix 1

ANALYSIS OF INPUT-OUTPUT DATA

A1.1 *Introduction*

Section A1.2 describes how the data from the 1975 input-output table are combined with time series data to examine trends in the different categories of imports over time. Section A1.3 describes the methodology used to analyse the tables and the source of these data is discussed in Section A1.4.

A1.2 *Input-Output Analysis*

The basic input-output table used is that described by Murphy (1984). The table, together with other related data, are stored on the CCS computer in the Department of Finance databank. Some preliminary transformations were carried out to eliminate duplication and to deal with the problem of negative stock changes. These transformations are described here. The derivation of the direct, indirect and total import contents of a unit of each component of final demand is also set out in this section. For these import contents to be used as propensities to import would require a range of very unrealistic assumptions to be valid (O'Connor and Henry, 1975):

(i)   ... each sector defined in the I/O table must produce a single output with a single input structure. There must be no possibility of substituting one input for another input in the production of a unit of output, i.e., the elasticity of substitution between any combination of inputs is zero. The volume of inputs does not vary with the level of output (constant returns to scale). There is no complementarity between the outputs of the different sectors. Together these imply that the technology of each sector can be represented by a Leontief or fixed coefficients production function.

(ii) The composition of each component of final demand which is treated as a separate variable (e.g., industrial exports) must be invariant with respect to the level of that variable.

For these coefficients to be equal to the propensity to import over a number of years would require that the fixed coefficients production function and the composition of each component of final demand remain invariant over time. While the unrealistic nature of these assumptions must be recognised, these data still have considerable value both in presenting a picture of the structure of the economy at a point in time and in providing a basis for further analysis of that structure. By disaggregating final demand into even smaller categories it is possible to reduce the problems arising from (ii) above. At the maximum level of disaggregation, where the output of each sector of final demand is separately identified, problems under (ii) can be eliminated. In this paper the approach adopted has been to disaggregate final demand into 20 different components and to weight each component by the propor-tion of the total accounted for, directly and indirectly, by the relevant category of imports. While this level of disaggregation of final demand will not totally eliminate the problems due to the unrealistic nature of assump-tion (ii), it should substantially reduce them. As a result, if assumption (i) were valid, the weighted final demand variable would be equal to, or at least close to, the actual volume of imports in each year. However, assumption (i) is clearly totally unrealistic and the observed differences between the weighted final demand variable and actual imports in each year will provide a crude measure of the extent to which assumption (i) is invalid.

On this basis, the change in the ratio of each component of imports to total final demand can be disaggregated into the effects of a shift in the com-position of final demand and a change due to all other factors (the invalidity of assumption (i)). The ratio of each component of imports to the weighted final demand variable should be largely purged of the compositional effect and, when suitably scaled, the difference between this ratio and the ratio of imports to unweighted final demand measures the change in the propensity to import due to compositional effects. The change in the ratio of imports to weighted final demand over time then measures the effects of all other variables, such as technical progress and substitution of factors in the pro-duction of each sector's output due to changes in the prices of those factors.

Viewed in another way these weighted final demand variables are an attempt to relax the assumption of strict input-output separability maintained by many other studies. They are used as an alternative activity variable in the different models of import demand estimated in Chapters 4 to 9. This variable allows the propensity to import out of each component of final demand to differ from the average propensity to import out of total final demand. The weighted final demand variable W is defined in A1.1:

$$W = \Sigma w_j F_j \tag{A1.1}$$

where F_j are the components of final demand and w_j are the weights derived from the I-O table and the demand equation for imports i is given by Equation A2.2:

$$M_i = W.F (P_k; \forall k = 1, n) \qquad (A1.2)$$

The propensity to import out of components F_j and F_1 of final demand are:

$$\frac{\delta M_i}{\delta F_j} = w_j.F \qquad \frac{\delta M_i}{\delta F_1} = w_1.F \qquad (A1.3)$$

The ratio of the two marginal propensities to import is fixed at w_j/w_1, the ratio of the two I-O coefficients. Thus, while somewhat less restrictive than the traditional approach of imposing input-output separability it still is quite restrictive. It is a matter for testing in the context of the different models whether it provides a more satisfactory representation of the data or whether further relaxations are necessary.

A1.3 *Methodology*

A detailed description of the methodology is given in O'Connor and Henry (1975) and Green (1976). The notation used is based on Green (1976).

(a) notation:

^ e.g. $\hat{W}$ The circumflex over the name of a vector means that the vector W has been converted into a diagonal matrix with the elements of W on the diagonal and zeros elsewhere.

'   W' The prime means that the vector or matrix W has been transposed.

U   is a unit vector of relevant size. Thus XU is a column vector the elements of which are the row totals of X.

I   is the identity matrix of relevant rank.

(b) variables

A precise description of the source of the variables is given in Section A1.4.

A   is a square matrix. The colums show the proportions of total inputs of each sector derived from every other sector.

F   is a matrix of primary inputs entering directly into each component of final demand.

P   is a matrix of the primary inputs into each sector of the economy. Rows one to six correspond to the six categories of imports modelled in the paper. (All imports are treated as primary inputs.)

T   is a vector of the total value of each of the components of final demand.

W   is a vector of gross outputs of each sector.
X   is a square matrix of the values of flows of intermediate consumption between each of the productive sectors.
Y   is a matrix of the values of final uses of each sector's output. The columns represent each of the categories of final demand, the rows correspond to each of the productive sectors of the economy.

(c)   definitions

$$X(\hat{W})^{-1} = A \tag{A1.4}$$

$$W = XU + YU \tag{A1.5}$$

$$T = UY + UF \tag{A1.6}$$

$$W = (UX + UP)' \tag{A1.7}$$

$$W = \hat{W}U \tag{A1.8}$$

From A1.4 $X = A\hat{W}$ (A1.9)

Taking A1.5 and substituting using A1.8 and A1.9

$$\hat{W}U = A\hat{W}U + YU \tag{A1.10}$$

Then:

$$(I-A)\hat{W}U = YU \tag{A1.11}$$

$$\hat{W}U = (I-A)^{-1}YU \tag{A1.12}$$

where

$(I-A)^{-1}Y$ is a matrix which shows the gross output content of a unit of each category of final demand. The rows represent the different categories of output, the columns, the different categories of demand.

$(I-A)^{-1}Y(\hat{T})^{-1}$ is the same as the previous matrix except that the gross output contents are expressed in coefficient form — showing the contents of a unit of each category of final demand.

$P(\hat{W})^{-1}$ is the matrix showing the primary input content of a unit of each category of output.

$F(\hat{T})^{-1}$ is the matrix showing the direct primary input content of each component of final demand in coefficient form.

$P(\hat{W})^{-1}(I-A)^{-1}Y(\hat{T})^{-1}$ is the matrix showing the indirect primary input content of a unit of each component of final demand (in coefficient form).

$(P(\hat{W})^{-1}(I-A)^{-1}Y +$
$F)(\hat{T})^{-1}$ is the matrix showing the total primary input content of a unit of each component of final demand.

In the case of the last three matrices, the direct, indirect and total import contents respectively of a unit of each component of final demand are shown in the first seven rows. These rows correspond to imports SITC 0 + 1, SITC 2 + 4, SITC 3, SITC 5-9, merchandise, services, total imports.

A1.4 *Source of Input-Output Data*

All the data used are derived from the I-O tables for 1975 produced by the CSO. The original transformations carried out are described in Murphy (1984) and the basic CSO I-O tables together with the tables transformed by Murphy are stored in the Department of Finance databank on the Department of the Public Service CCS computer. They are archived in that databank under the name "IO". The data were further transformed, as described below, before carrying out the analysis set out in the previous sections. The full set of data are available from the author. While the 1975 I-O table is now twelve years old it is the latest available from the CSO. Although some tables have been produced by Henry (1986) for later years these involve a substantial amount of estimation and they are not available in the required format or with the required level of detail.

Variable used in this study	Variable derived from archive IO	Derivation
Y	FD-ADJ28	formed by taking the columns of FD-ADJ28 in the following order: 1 to 9, 21, 22, 14, 18, 19, 20+23, 24, 15, 12, 13, 11. Column 21 contains the sum across these rows.
F	FD-PIADJ28	formed in the same way as Y.
X	A-ADJ	No change.
P	PA-D	formed by taking the rows of PA-D in the following order: 1 to 4, sum of 1 to 4, 5, sum of 1 to 5, 6, 7, sum of 6 and 7, 8 to 12, sum of 8 to 12, sum of 1, to 12.

Set out below is a summary of the sectors of the resulting X matrix:

1	S01	Agric., For., Fish.
2	S03	Coal + Briquettes
3	S05	Coke prods.
4	S09	Petroleum prods.
5	S11	Elec, Gas, Water
6	S13	Metals + Ores
7	S15	O/Mineral prods.
8	S17	Chem. prods.
9	S19	Metal prods.
10	S21	Agr. + Ind. mach.
11	S23	Office Mach. + Instrument engineering
12	S25	Elec. goods
13	S27	Motor vehicles
14	S29	O/Transport equip.
15	S31	Meat processing, etc.
16	S33	Milk + Dairy prods.
17	S35	O/Food prods.
18	S37	Beverages
19	S39	Tobacco
20	S41	Textiles + Clothing
21	S43	Leather + Footwear
22	S45	Timber + Furniture
23	S47	Paper + Printing
24	S49	Rubber + Plastics
25	S51	O/Manufacturing
26	S53	Building + Const.
27	S55	Recovery + Repair
28	S57	Wholesale + Retail
29	S59	Lodging + Catering
30	S61	Inland transport
31	S63	Sea + Air transport
32	S65	Auxil. transport
33	S67	Communications
34	S69	Credit + Insurance
35	S71	Business services
36	S73	Rent of immov. goods
37	S79	O/Mkt. services
38	S81	General government
39	S89	Non-Mkt. health
40	S93	Educ. + O/Non-Mkt. serv.

Set out below is the order of the columns in the resulting Y matrix:

1 Food	12 Public authorities' consumption
2 Drink	13 Investment, building
3 Tobacco	14 Investment, other
4 Clothing + Footwear	15 Change in stocks — agriculture
5 Fuel	16 Change in stocks — other
6 Petrol	17 Change in stocks — intervention
7 Durables	18 Ag. exports
8 Transport equipment	19 Ind. exports
9 Exp. abrd.	20 Ser. exports
10 Consumption, other goods	21 Total
11 Consumption, other services	

Set out below is the order of the rows of the resulting P matrix:

1 Merch. imp 0/1	5 Merch. imp total
2 Merch. imp 2-4	6 Ser. imp.
3 Merch. imp 3	7 Total imports
4 Merch. imp 5-9	8 Indirect tax

9 Subsidy   14 O/Profits
10 Ind. tax-subs.   15 O/Deprec.
11 Wages   16 Net output
12 Ag. profits   17 Total primary
13 Ag. deprec.

Appendix 2

DERIVATION OF ELASTICITIES FROM GENERALISED LEONTIEF COST FUNCTIONS

The elasticities are derived for the "basic" model, Equation 2.16 in Chapter 2.

$$M_i = W[\sum_j b_{ij} (P_j/P_i)^{\frac{1}{2}} + \sum_k C_{ik} (x_k/p_i)^{\frac{1}{2}} + b_{it} T + b_{id} D + b_{ic} CAPQ]/2 \quad (A2.1)$$

Differentiating Equation A2.1 with respect to the own price P_i:

$$\frac{\delta M_i}{\delta P_i} = W[\sum_j b_{ij} (P_j/P_i)^{\frac{1}{2}} + \sum_k C_{ik} (x_k/P_i)^{\frac{1}{2}}]/(4P_i) \quad (A2.2)$$
$$i \neq j$$

The own price elasticity e_{ii} is:

$$e_{ii} = \frac{\delta M_i}{\delta P_i} \cdot \frac{P_i}{M_i} = W[\sum_j b_{ij} (P_j/P_i)^{\frac{1}{2}} + \sum_k C_{ik} (x_k/P_i)^{\frac{1}{2}}]/(4M_i)(\quad (A2.3)$$
$$i \neq j$$

The price elasticity with respect to the price of another variable factor P_j, e_{ij}, is:

$$e_{ij} = \frac{\delta M_i}{\delta P_j} \cdot \frac{P_j}{M_i} = Wb_{ij} (p_j/p_i)^{\frac{1}{2}}/(4.M_i) \quad (A2.4)$$

The elasticity with respect to a change in one of the fixed factors x_k, e_{ik}, is:

$$e_{ik} = \frac{\delta M_i}{\delta x_k} \cdot \frac{x_k}{M_i} = WC_{ik} (x_k/p_i)^{\frac{1}{2}} \bar{\jmath} (4.M_i) \quad (A2.5)$$

The variance and standard error for each elasticity can be derived from the variance of each of the estimated parameters b_{ij} and C_{ik} where the elasticity e is a function of these parameters:

$$e = F(b_{ij}, c_{ik} ; \forall i,j,k)$$

using the formula

$$\text{var}(e) = (\delta F/\delta x)\, V(\delta F/\delta x)' \tag{A2.6}$$

where V is the matrix of the variance of the parameters.

This requires information on the differential of each elasticity with respect to each parameter. These are shown below. The variance matrix V is obtained from the estimation of Equation A2.1.

$$\frac{\delta e_{ii}}{\delta b_{ii}} = 0 \tag{A2.7}$$

$$\frac{\delta e_{ii}}{\delta b_{ij}} = W(P_j/P_i)^{\frac{1}{2}}/(4\,M_i) \tag{A2.8}$$
$$i \neq j$$

$$\frac{\delta e_{ii}}{\delta C_{ik}} = W(x_k/P_i)^{\frac{1}{2}}/(4.M_i) \tag{A2.9}$$

$$\frac{\delta e_{ij}}{\delta b_{ii}} = 0 \tag{A2.10}$$

$$\frac{\delta e_{ij}}{\delta b_{ij}} = W(p_j/p_i)^{\frac{1}{2}}/(4.M_i) \tag{A2.11}$$
$$i \neq j$$

$$\frac{\delta e_{ij}}{\delta b_{il}} = 0 \tag{A2.12}$$
$$1 \neq i \neq j$$

$$\frac{\delta e_{ij}}{\delta C_{ik}} = 0 \tag{A2.13}$$

$$\frac{\delta e_{ik}}{\delta C_{ik}} = W(x_k/P_i)^{\frac{1}{2}}/(4.M_i) \tag{A2.14}$$

$$\frac{\delta e_{ik}}{\delta b_{ij}} = 0 \tag{A2.15}$$

$$\frac{\delta e_{ik}}{\delta C_{il}} = 0 \tag{A2.16}$$
$$1 \neq k$$

From Equations A2.10 to A2.12 it is clear that the standard error of the elasticity with respect to the price of a variable input P_j (not the own price), is solely dependent on the standard error of the coefficient b_{ij}. As a result, the standard t test on that coefficient tests the significance of the elasticity e_{ij}. A similar situation holds with respect to the elasticity with respect to the fixed inputs. However, the standard error of the own price elasticity is a function of the standard errors of the coefficients b_{ij} $(i{\neq}j)$ and C_{ik}.

Appendix 3

DERIVATION OF ELASTICITIES FOR THE AIDS MODEL

The basic AIDS model is as follows:

$$w_i = a_i + \sum_j c_{ij} \log p_j + b_i \log(x/p) \qquad (A3.1)$$

where w_i = the share of the value of consumption of good i in the value of total consumption,

x = the value of total consumption (which is equal to the cost function),

p_j = the price of good j.

The implicit aggregate price index is of the form:

$$\log p = d + \sum_i a_i \log p_i + \tfrac{1}{2}\sum_i \sum_j c_{ij} \log p_i \log p_j \qquad (A3.2)$$

For the purpose of estimation the aggregate price index defined in Equation A3.2 is approximated by the price index defined in Equation A3.3:

$$\log p = \sum_i w_i \log p_i \qquad (A3.3)$$

This is, in fact, very close to the implicit price deflator for personal consumption. Equation A3.1 can be rewritten using Equation A3.2 as follows:

$$q_i = x/p_i \left[a_i + \sum_j c_{ij} \log p_j + b_i \log x - b_i d \right.$$

$$\left. - b_i \sum_k a_k \log p_k - \tfrac{1}{2} b_i \sum_k \sum_j c_{kj} \log p_k \log p_j \right] \qquad (A3.4)$$

where q_i = the volume of consumption of good i.

The elasticity of demand for good i with respect to its own price, e_{ii}, is defined as:

$$e_{ii} = (\delta q_i/\delta p_i)\,(p_i/q_i) = p_i/q_i\,[-q_i/p_i + (c_{ii}/p_i)(x/p_i)$$
$$- (x/p_i)\,b_i a_i/p_i - (x/p_i)\,b_i \Sigma c_{ij}\,\log p_j/p_i] \qquad (A3.5)$$

$$e_{ii} = [c_{ii} - w_i\,(1 + b_i) + b_i^2\,\log\,(x/p)]/w_i \qquad (A3.6)$$

The cross price elasticity, e_{ij}, is defined as:

$$e_{ij} = (\delta q_i/\delta p_j)\,(p_j/q_i) = p_j/q_i\,(x/p_i)\,[c_{ij} - b_i a_j - b_i\,\Sigma c_{kj}\log p_k]/p_j \qquad (A3.7)$$

$$e_{ij} = [c_{ij} - b_i w_j + b_i b_j\,\log\,(x/p)]/w_i \qquad (A3.8)$$

The budget elasticity, e_i, is defined as:

$$e_i = (\delta q_i/\delta x)\,(x/q_i) = 1 + (x/w_i)\,(b_i/x) \qquad (A3.9)$$

$$e_i = 1 + b_i/w_i \qquad (A3.10)$$

The variance and standard error for each elasticity can be derived from the variance of each of the estimated parameters z where the elasticity e is a function of these parameters:

$$e = F(z) \qquad (A3.11)$$

using the formula

$$\text{var}(e) = (\delta F/\delta z)\,V\,(\delta F/\delta z)' \qquad (A3.12)$$

where V is the matrix with the variance of the parameters on the diagonal. This requires information on the differential of each elasticity with respect to each parameter. These are shown below on the assumption that symmetry aggregation and homogeneity are not imposed on the system of demand equations. The variance matrix V is obtained from the estimation of Equation A3.1.

As a first step it is useful to differentiate q_i with respect to each of the coefficients.

$$\delta q_i/\delta c_{ij} = (x/p_i)\,(\log p_j - b_i\,\log p_i\,\log p_j) \qquad (A3.13)$$
$$\delta q_i/\delta b_i = (x/p_i)\,(\log x - \log p) \qquad (A3.14)$$
$$\delta q_i/\delta a_i = (x/p_i)\,(1 - b_i\,\log p_i) \qquad (A3.15)$$

If one ignores the differential of q_i with respect to the other parameters which will have a very small effect on the eventual result one gets the following set of equations from Equation A3.5:

$$\delta e_{ii}/\delta c_{ii} = - [(1 + e_{ii}) (\log p_i - b_i (\log p_i)^2) - 1 + b_i \log p_i]/w_i \quad (A3.16)$$

$$\delta e_{ii}/\delta c_{ij} = - [(1 + e_{ii}) (\log p_j - b_i (\log p_i.\log p_j)) + b_i \log p_j]/w_i \quad (A3.17)$$

$$\delta e_{ii}/\delta b_i = - [(1 + e_{ii}) \log (x/p) + (w_i - b_i \log (x/p))]/w_i \quad (A3.18)$$

$$\delta e_{ii}/\delta a_i = - [(1 + e_{ii}) (1 - b_i \log p_i) + b_i]/w_i \quad (A3.19)$$

$$\delta e_{ij}/\delta c_{ij} = - [e_{ij} (\log p_j - b_i \log p_i \log p_j) + 1 - b_i \log p_i]/w_i \quad (A3.20)$$

$$\delta e_{ij}/\delta c_{ik} = - e_{ij} [(\log p_k - b_i \log p_i \log p_k)]/w_i \quad (A3.21)$$
$$j \neq k$$

$$\delta e_{ij}/\delta b_i = - [e_{ij} \log (x/p) + a_j + \Sigma c_{kj} \log p_k]/w_i \quad (A3.22)$$

$$\delta e_{ij}/\delta a_i = - [e_{ij} (1 - b_i \log p_i) + b_i]/w_i \quad (A3.23)$$

$$\delta e_i/\delta c_{ii} = - b_i [\log p_i - b_i (\log p_i)^2]/w_i^2 \quad (A3.24)$$

$$\delta e_i/\delta c_{ij} = - b_i [\log p_j - b_i \log p_i \log p_j]/w_i^2 \quad (A3.25)$$

$$\delta e_i/\delta b_i = [w_i - b_i \log (x/p)]/w_i^2 \quad (A3.26)$$

$$\delta e_i/\delta a_i = - [b_i (1 - b_i \log p_i)]/w_i^2 \quad (A3.27)$$

ESRI PUBLICATIONS

Books:

Economic Growth in Ireland: The Experience Since 1947
Kieran A. Kennedy and Brendan Dowling

Irish Economic Policy: A Review of Major Issues
Staff Members of ESRI (eds. B. R. Dowling and J. Durkan)

The Irish Economy and Society in the 1980s (Papers presented at ESRI Twenty-first Anniversary Conference)
Staff Members of ESRI

The Economic and Social State of The Nation
J. F. Meenan, M. P. Fogarty, J. Kavanagh and L. Ryan

The Irish Economy: Policy and Performance 1972-1981
P. Bacon, J. Durkan and J. O'Leary

Employment and Unemployment Policy for Ireland
Staff Members of ESRI (eds., Denis Conniffe and Kieran A. Kennedy)

Public Social Expenditure – Value for Money? (Papers presented at a Conference, 20. November 1984)

Medium-Term Outlook: 1986-1990. No. 1   Peter Bacon

Ireland in Transition   Kieran A. Kennedy (ed.)

Policy Research Series:

1. *Regional Policy and the Full-Employment Target*   M. Ross and B. Walsh
2. *Energy Demand in Ireland, Projections and Policy Issues*   S. Scott
3. *Some Issues in the Methodology of Attitude Research*   E. E. Davis *et al.*
4. *Land Drainage Policy in Ireland*   Richard Bruton and Frank J. Convery
5. *Recent Trends in Youth Unemployment*   J. J. Sexton
6. *The Economic Consequences of European Union. A Symposium on Some Policy Aspects*
D. Scott, J. Bradley, J. D. FitzGerald and M. Ross
7. *The National Debt and Economic Policy in the Medium Term*   John D. FitzGerald

Broadsheet Series:

1. *Dental Services in Ireland*   P. R. Kaim-Caudle
2. *We Can Stop Rising Prices*   M. P. Fogarty
3. *Pharmaceutical Services in Ireland*   P. R. Kaim-Caudle
assisted by Annette O'Toole and Kathleen O'Donoghue
4. *Ophthalmic Services in Ireland*   P. R. Kaim-Caudle
assisted by Kathleen O'Donoghue and Annette O'Toole
5. *Irish Pensions Schemes, 1969*   P. R. Kaim-Caudle and J. G. Byrne
assisted by Annette O'Toole
6. *The Social Science Percentage Nuisance*   R. C. Geary
7. *Poverty in Ireland: Research Priorities*   Brendan M. Walsh
8. *Irish Entrepreneurs Speak for Themselves*   M. P. Fogarty
9. *Marital Desertion in Dublin: An Exploratory Study*   Kathleen O'Higgins
10. *Equalization of Opportunity in Ireland: Statistical Aspects*
R. C. Geary and F. S. Ó Muircheartaigh
11. *Public Social Expenditure in Ireland*   Finola Kennedy
12. *Problems in Economic Planning and Policy Formation in Ireland, 1958–1974*
Desmond Norton
13. *Crisis in the Cattle Industry*   R. O'Connor and P. Keogh
14. *A Study of Schemes for the Relief of Unemployment in Ireland*
R. C. Geary and M. Dempsey
    with Appendix   E. Costa
15. *Dublin Simon Community, 1971-1976: An Exploration*   Ian Hart

16. *Aspects of the Swedish Economy and their Relevance to Ireland*
Robert O'Connor, Eoin O'Malley and Anthony Foley
17. *The Irish Housing System: A Critical Overview*
T. J. Baker and L. M. O'Brien
18. *The Irish Itinerants: Some Demographic, Economic and Educational Aspects*
M. Dempsey and R. C. Geary
19. *A Study of Industrial Workers' Co-operatives*
Robert O'Connor and Philip Kelly
20. *Drinking in Ireland: A Review of Trends in Alcohol Consumption, Alcohol Related Problems and Policies towards Alcohol* Brendan M. Walsh
21. *A Review of the Common Agricultural Policy and the Implications of Modified Systems for Ireland* R. O'Connor, C. Guiomard and J. Devereux
22. *Policy Aspects of Land-Use Planning in Ireland*
Frank J. Convery and A. Allan Schmid
23. *Issues in Adoption in Ireland* Harold J. Abramson

Geary Lecture Series:
1. *A Simple Approach to Macro-economic Dynamics* (1967)   R. G. D. Allen
2. *Computers, Statistics and Planning-Systems or Chaos?* (1968)   F. G. Foster
3. *The Dual Career Family* (1970)   Rhona and Robert Rapoport
4. *The Psychosonomics of Rising Prices* (1971)   H. A. Turner
5. *An Interdisciplinary Approach to the Measurement of Utility or Welfare* (1972)
J. Tinbergen
6. *Econometric Forecasting from Lagged Relationships* (1973)   M. G. Kendall
7. *Towards a New Objectivity* (1974)   Alvin W. Gouldner
8. *Structural Analysis in Sociology* (1975)   Robert K. Merton
9. *British Economic Growth 1951-1973: Success or Failure?* (1976)
R. C. O. Matthews
10. *Official Statisticians and Econometricians in the Present Day World* (1977)
E. Malinvaud
11. *Political and Institutional Economics* (1978)   Gunnar Myrdal
12. *The Dilemmas of a Socialist Economy: The Hungarian Experience* (1979)
János Kornai
13. *The Story of a Social Experiment and Some Reflections* (1980)
Robert M. Solow
14. *Modernisation and Religion* (1981)   P. L. Berger
15. *Poor, Relatively Speaking* (1983)   Amartya K. Sen
16. *Towards More Rational Decisions on Criminals* (1984)   Daniel Glaser
17. *An Economic Analysis of the Family* (1985)   Gary S. Becker

General Research Series:
1. *The Ownership of Personal Property in Ireland*   Edward Nevin
2. *Short-Term Economic Forecasting and its Application in Ireland*   Alfred Kuehn
3. *The Irish Tariff and The E.E.C.: A Factual Survey*   Edward Nevin
4. *Demand Relationships for Ireland*   C. E. V. Leser
5. *Local Government Finance in Ireland: A Preliminary Survey*   David Walker
6. *Prospects of the Irish Economy in 1962*   Alfred Kuehn
7. *The Irish Woollen and Worsted Industry, 1946-59: A Study in StatisticalMethod*
R. C. Geary

ESRI PUBLICATIONS

ESRI PUBLICATIONS

ESRI PUBLICATIONS

ESRI PUBLICATIONS